GATEWAY OF LIFE

▟ Foundations series

Testifying to the faith and creativity of the Orthodox Christian
Church, the Foundations series draws upon the riches of its
tradition to address the modern world. These survey texts are
suitable both for preliminary inquiry and deeper investigation,
in the classroom and for personal study.

Peter C. Bouteneff
Series Editor

Gateway of Life

ORTHODOX THINKING ON THE MOTHER OF GOD

Mary B. Cunningham

ST VLADIMIR'S SEMINARY PRESS
YONKERS, NY 10707
2015

Library of Congress Cataloging-in-Publication Data

Cunningham, Mary.
    Gateway of life : Orthodox thinking on the Mother of God / Mary B.
Cunningham.
        pages cm   — (Foundations series, ISSN 1556–9837 ; book 7)
    Includes bibliographical references.
    ISBN 978–0–88141–524–7 (paper)— ISBN 978–0–88141–525–4 (electronic)
    1. Mary, Blessed Virgin, Saint.   2. Orthodox Eastern Church—
Doctrines.   I. Title.

BT610.C866 2015
232.91—dc23

                                                        2015024669

© 2015 BY MARY B. CUNNINGHAM

ST VLADIMIR'S SEMINARY PRESS
575 Scarsdale Rd, Yonkers, NY 10707
1–800–204–2665
www.svspress.com

ISSN 1556–9837
ISBN 978–0–88141–524–7 (paper)
ISBN 978–0–88141–525–4 (electronic)

PRINTED IN THE UNITED STATES OF AMERICA

For
Richard, Emily, and James

CONTENTS

FOREWORD

The Bible, taken on its own, gives us little information about Mary, the virgin who bore and gave birth to Jesus Christ. Yet throughout the history of the Christian Church she has been the focus of unparalleled love and devotion, the subject of fervent prayer. For countless people she is the heavenly mother, the first one to turn to with their urgent hopes and desperate needs. To add to this, she has been the subject of significant debate over the centuries, concerning theology as well as devotion. Theologically, there were ancient questions centered on the person of Christ, whom she bore in her womb. More recently, many Christians as well as non-Christians are puzzled: What in the Bible gives us the foundation for this degree of attention to Mary? Is not her veneration a potentially dangerous exaggeration, akin to goddess-worship? Is it not God, and His Christ and His Spirit, that are our proper focuses?

Such questions arise especially in the churches born of the Reformation, although they can emanate also from people within churches where she is deeply venerated. It is not always easy to answer such queries, as the heartfelt love surrounding our experience of Mary makes it impossible fully to explain and still less feasible to convince someone of it. Yet we can learn a great deal from an informed and engaged exploration of the ways Mary, the Mother of God, has been understood in the Church. This book, by a scholar and person of faith, provides exactly that.

The questions about Mary continue to be both theological and devotional; they concern what the Church teaches about her and how Christians express their love for her. This book wisely chooses not to treat these two as utterly distinct spheres. Just as it would be misleading to make a clean divide between "the head" and "the heart"—even as we can identify different emphases and approaches—so it would be wrong to say that the dogma about Mary is cleanly distinct from our personal, spiritual relationship with her and the hope we place in her.

This is because theology is properly a *holistic* enterprise. That means two things. One is that you cannot set "Mariology," or any other subject, apart from other subjects, because they all affect each other, and ultimately find their coherence in Jesus Christ. The other is that theology is not merely an intellectual exercise. It stems from and leads to a fully-realized Christian life. Theology affects our prayer life, our moral stances, and our love for one another and for the created world. And vice-versa. Moreover, theology is inextricably involved with the Liturgy: what we believe is what we pray. And vice-versa. The Liturgy itself is by definition a holistic endeavor, to which we bring our hearts, minds, and bodies.

For us to learn about the history and the substance of the veneration of the Mother of God will therefore enrich our whole Christian life. So will our loving immersion in the Church's liturgical life. In all this, we will also increase our knowledge of Jesus Christ, whom she bore and raised. To call her "the mother of *God*" is to acknowledge Jesus' identity as divine: the Son of God the Father. But it also shows his identity as human, for she imparted to him his own full and complete humanity; she is the source of his human composition. Calling her "Theotokos" or "Mother of God" is therefore limitlessly profound.

She is also called "Ever-Virgin." Like "Theotokos," this title has profound implication for our understanding of Christ's identity. Mary conceived Christ without a human father. Had it been otherwise, if he had an earthly father (such as Joseph or a Roman centurion), Jesus would have been a new person who had not existed before the first century AD. But he did not come into existence with his conception in Mary's womb—he was and is the ever-existing Son of the ever-existing Father.

Mary was indeed a virgin and remained one throughout her life. Just as a temple is consecrated for one use and one alone, her womb—the temple of God—was devoted to that sole purpose. She is therefore Ever-Virgin; her body, soul, and mind were given over to bearing God. It follows that the Church venerates her as "all-pure," and "all-holy," in a very particular way.

So she continues to be venerated not only for her role in Christ's life—and therefore as the ladder between earth and heaven—but also for her own virtues. Some of the countless prayers and hymns to Mary focus on her purity, her tenderness, her wisdom, her love and intercession for us before her Son, while others focus on the divine-human (theanthropic) identity of her Son. One example brings together a precise, even technical-sounding theological concept of Christ's identity with a fervent call for her intercession:

> How shall we not marvel at your divine-human
>   childbearing, all-honored one?
> For without receiving the touch of a man, all-blameless
>   one,

you brought into the world a Son in the flesh without a
 father,
the One begotten from the Father before the ages without
 a mother.
He admitted of no change or mixture or division,
but rather guarded surely what is particular to each
 nature.
Wherefore entreat him, O Lady and Virgin Mother,
to save the souls of those who make the Orthodox
 confession of you as the Mother of God.[1]

Mary has long been and continues to be central to Orthodox
Christian life. In this, the Orthodox share a great deal of common ground with Roman Catholics and many Anglicans, though,
as this book shows, there are also some significant distinctions.
This study aims to provide a fuller comprehension of her identity
and how she has been understood in the wider Church through
its history. May such comprehension be in the service of a closer
relationship with Mary, the All-Holy Mother of God, and for
the one whom she bore and to whom she prays for us, our Lord
Jesus Christ.

—Peter Bouteneff

[1]Tone 3 Resurrectional Dogmatikon.

INTRODUCTION

Mary occupies a central place in Orthodox Christian tradition. If someone were to enter an Orthodox church for the first time and to participate not only in a Divine Liturgy but also in one of the offices (such as Vespers or Matins), he or she would be struck by the constant invocations of this holy figure, who is called the "All-Pure Virgin" and "Mother of God." Short hymns, known as "theotokia," are found throughout the liturgical services; occasionally there will also be a recitation of the "Magnificat" or a statement of faith, framed in a hymn to the Mother of God, called a "dogmatikon." In the Divine Liturgy, the holy "anaphora," or consecration of the Eucharist, closes with an invocation to the Virgin Mary when the choir sings the following words:

> It is truly right to call you blessed, who gave birth to God, ever blessed and most pure, and Mother of our God. Greater in honor than the Cherubim and beyond compare more glorious than the Seraphim, without corruption you gave birth to God the Word; truly the Mother of God, we magnify you.[1]

Orthodox Christians also pray to the Mother of God in their homes, addressing icons that depict her as "The Sign," "The

---

[1]Archimandrite Ephrem Lash, trans., *The Divine Liturgy of our Father among the Saints John Chrysostom*, The Greek Orthodox Diocese of Thyateira and Great Britain (Chipping Norton: Nigel Lynn Publishing, 2011), 47.

Merciful One," and in other aspects. Such iconography, which usually shows Mary with the infant Christ in her arms, has ancient origins according to tradition: the Virgin as "Hodegetria," or "Guide," for example, is believed to be based on an image that was painted by the Evangelist Luke. Many Orthodox will also address the Mother of God as they work or travel: she is the blessed "Panagia" or "All-holy One," who watches over them and comes to their aid at difficult moments in their lives.

The Church has always ensured, by means of hymns, sermons, and catechetical texts, that Orthodox Christians remember the doctrinal reasons for their veneration of the Mother of God. She played a central role in the mystery of the Incarnation, having been chosen by God as the virgin mother of his Son, Jesus Christ, according to Old Testament prophecy (especially Is 7.14). This was not a passive process, however; Orthodox tradition stresses the fact that Mary freely chose to accept this role when she gave her answer to the archangel Gabriel, saying, "Let it be to me according to your word" (Lk 1.38). Orthodox Christian icons, hymns, and other liturgical texts stress the Virgin's importance in the Christological mystery, even when they are also invoking her intercessory and protective powers.

Mary, the Mother of God, is a figure who has many dimensions, as we shall see in the course of this book. She is the "All-Holy" ("Panagia") Virgin, the "Second Eve," intercessor, and Mother of God ("Mētēr Theou"), as well as being "Birth-giver of God" ("Theotokos"). Some of these roles developed in Christian consciousness later than others: for example, whereas Mary is frequently called "Theotokos" in texts dated to the fourth century, her epithet "Mother of God" only came into regular use from about the ninth century onward.[2] Liturgical texts employ many names, showing constantly that Mary embodies different aspects of God's intention for human salvation. One of the most revealing Biblical texts concerning the Virgin Mary is her "Magnificat," in which she prays for the lowly to be exalted and the hungry to be filled with good things (Lk 1.52–53). The Mother of God is all things to all people, but she especially offers hope to the ordinary—and sometimes down-trodden—Christians who are most in need of help.

How this Book is Organized

I have chosen to organize this book thematically, with chapters focusing on separate aspects of the Virgin Mary's place in Orthodox tradition, but also with attention to their historical development. The book is thus divided into eight chapters, not counting the Introduction and Conclusion.

In Chapter One, we explore the most authoritative sources or revelation concerning the Mother of God, namely Christian Scripture, which includes the Old and New Testaments. The Bible is the source for much reflection on Mary, which is manifested in her feasts, in theological writings, and in icons. Orthodox Christianity has always used the version of the Old Testament that is known as the Septuagint. This is a Greek translation of the Hebrew Bible, which Christians believe to be inspired by the Holy Spirit. It differs in some ways from the Hebrew Bible, but it is probably the text that the New Testament writers knew and used. The Old Testament provided the basis for their interpretation of

[2]See I. Kalavrezou, "When the Virgin Mary became *Meter Theou*," *Dumbarton Oaks Papers* 44 (1990), 165–72.

Jesus Christ's Incarnation, Passion, and Resurrection, along with the Virgin Mary's important role in these events.

Chapter Two, building on the Biblical basis, examines the so-called "apocryphal," or non-canonical, traditions surrounding the Mother of God. Such texts began to appear in the course of the second century and continued to be written, not only in Greek but also in many other languages too, throughout the medieval period. Although excluded from the Biblical canon because they were not formally associated with the first apostles, some of these works have been accepted into Orthodox Christian tradition. The feast of the Nativity of the Mother of God (September 8), for example, is based on the second-century text known as the *Protevangelium of James*, which provides an account of her conception, infancy, and betrothal to Joseph. That of Mary's Dormition or "Falling Asleep" (August 15) follows accounts of her death and assumption into heaven that began to be written down in the course of the fifth century. Such sources have been embraced by the Orthodox Church both because they describe aspects of Mary's life that are not covered in Scripture, but also because they provide further theological reflection on her role in the mystery of the Incarnation of Christ.

Chapter Three turns to the theme of the Virgin Mary as the "Second Eve," which developed in the course of the second century. This theme complements, or presages, that of Christ as the "Second Adam," according to Irenaeus of Lyons' doctrine of "recapitulation." By using the gift of free will to obey rather than disobey God, Mary opened the way to the restoration of grace in humanity and in creation; this process was fulfilled when Christ became incarnate in her womb "in the image and according to the likeness of God" (Gen 1.26).

In Chapter Four, we examine the meaning of Mary's virginity in both moral and theological terms. This theme has importance both with regard to the historical narrative of Mary's upbringing and character, but also in relation to her role as Birth-Giver or Mother of God.

Chapter Five moves on to the place of Mary, the Theotokos, in Christological doctrine, which was debated and formally defined in the course of the fifth century AD. The acceptance of the title "Theotokos" ("Birth-giver of God") had significant implications not only for Mary but also for Christ, who was recognized as being fully divine (as the Son of God) as well as fully human (as the Son of Mary)—a teaching that came to be expressed in terms of Christ's "two natures," divine and human.

In Chapter Six, we turn to Mary's role as mediator and protector of the Christian faithful. A wealth of evidence, both textual and material, survives from the medieval and modern periods, testifying to the continuing presence and intercession of the Mother of God in creation. Once it did emerge, the intercessory role of the Mother of God became an important feature of Church tradition and remains so to this day.

Chapter Seven deals with more modern perceptions of the Mother of God, including the view of nineteenth- and early twentieth-century Russian Sophiologists, that she represents an important symbol of the cosmic "feminine" principle in Orthodox tradition. The contributions of theologians including Elisabeth Behr-Sigel, Vladimir Lossky, Metropolitan Kallistos Ware, and others will also be considered in this chapter.

Finally, in Chapter Eight, we consider the similarities and differences that exist between Eastern and Western Christian views of the Mother of God. Variations in dogma concerning her conception and assumption into heaven require explanation here; these stem, in part, from different understandings of the human condition and original, or ancestral, sin. There are nevertheless grounds for common understanding between the two traditions since both revere Mary's purity and motherhood of Christ, the Son of God. However, some stumbling blocks, especially in the form of papal bulls published between 1854 and 1950, remain. This chapter will also explore the possibility of shared positions between Christianity and the other two Abrahamic religions, Judaism and Islam, with respect to the Virgin Mary. There are already signs that contact is being made between believers as well as scholars in these three religious traditions; while fundamental differences will remain, it is possible to acknowledge common expressions of devotion to the Virgin Mary.

A brief Conclusion draws together the various themes that have been explored in this book. While the diverse strands that contribute to the Orthodox understanding of the Mother of God developed at somewhat different times, ecclesial tradition assimilates them in a coherent way. Hymns, sermons, icons, and narratives portray many aspects of the Mother of God, often simultaneously. This may be illustrated by the following short hymn, or *dogmatikon*, which belongs to the office of Small Vespers, Tone One:

> O Virgin: the Prophet named you Cloud of eternal light, for the Word of the Father, Christ our God, descending from you like rain upon a fleece and dawning from you, has enlightened the world and destroyed error. Do not cease

to intercede insistently we pray, all-holy Lady, for us who acknowledge you to be true Mother of God.[3]

Why This Book?

Before embarking on this short study of the Mother of God in Orthodox tradition, it is worth asking whether there is actually a need for it. A few excellent books by Orthodox writers already exist on this subject, including those by George S. Gabriel, St John Maximovitch, Jaroslav Pelikan, and Alexander Schmemann.[4] This book builds on the foundations established by these works. It is also written in a style that is intended to be informative and easy to understand. However, in contrast to previous studies by Orthodox Christian writers, the present book adopts a more historical approach to the subject. It thus explores some topics that have not previously been addressed fully, such as the ways in which canonical and apocryphal sources interact in Orthodox Christian tradition and how we should interpret non-biblical texts such as the *Protevangelium of James*. It is likely that the *Protevangelium* was written primarily in order to uphold, by means of a highly symbolic (while also biblically inspired) narrative, the reality of Christ's virgin birth from a mother whose purity and holiness

[3]Trans. Archimandrite Ephrem Lash at <http://www.anastasis.org.uk/sat1ec. htm>.

[4]George S. Gabriel, *Mary. The Untrodden Portal of God* (Ridgewood, NJ: Zephyr Publishing, 2nd ed., 2005); Blessed Archbishop John Maximovitch, *The Orthodox Veneration of the Mother of God* (Platina, CA: St Herman of Alaska Brotherhood, 1987); Jaroslav Pelikan, *Mary Through the Centuries: Her Place in the History of Culture* (New Haven, CT and London: Yale University Press, 1996); Alexander Schmemann, *The Virgin Mary, Celebration of Faith*, vol. 3 (Crestwood, NY; St Vladimir's Seminary Press, 2001).

had remained intact from the moment of her own miraculous (although not virgin) birth. Searching for the historical Mary, who undoubtedly did lead a humble life in Palestine as the wife of the carpenter Joseph, represents only one small aspect of the role that she came to assume for Christians in both Eastern and Western Christendom.

Texts thus need to be considered both with respect to their historical and cultural backgrounds and on the basis of their underlying agendas. As Father John Behr has suggested in relation to the New Testament, this holy book should be read against the background of a Christian community that believed firmly in the Resurrection of Christ.[5] That is the message that motivated the Evangelists and St Paul in their writing of the Gospels and Epistles for Jews and Gentiles. Texts concerning the Mother of God also have an underlying agenda. This means that we should attempt to understand what motivated their writers and why certain aspects of Mary's person, such as her virginity or intercessory qualities, were stressed more by some than by others.

Orthodox tradition is seamless in the sense that the Church has always attempted to incorporate those elements of faith that have truly been affirmed on the basis of discerning prayer and with the guidance of the Holy Spirit. However, this process took place slowly in the course of the centuries, sometimes in response to theological controversy or to external pressures. It is acceptable, in my view, to study this process and to attempt to unravel the

[5]See, for example, John Behr's Preface to *The Mystery of Christ. Life in Death* (Crestwood, NY: St Vladimir's Seminary Press, 2006), 15–20, but also his earlier works, *The Way to Nicaea* (Crestwood, NY: St Vladimir's Seminary Press, 2001) and *The Nicene Faith* (Crestwood, NY: St Vladimir's Seminary Press, 2004).

various strands that eventually came together to form the rich portrayal of Mary, the Mother of God, that we find in Orthodox hymnography and iconography. I also hope that certain topics, such as the differences between Western and Orthodox dogma and the possibility for ecumenical dialogue, will profit from fresh treatment. Above all, and against the background of a growing body of publications on the Virgin Mary that has been produced especially by Roman Catholic scholars,[6] I hope that one small offering that is written from an Orthodox perspective will prove useful and illuminating.

I would like to thank the editor of the Foundations series, Dr Peter Bouteneff, for his meticulous editing of the book, as well as for his generous Foreword. Thanks are also due to Fr Benedict Churchill, who proof-read the text and offered valuable comments. I assume full responsibility for any errors that remain.

Further Reading:

Boss, Sarah Jane, ed. *Mary: The Complete Resource*. London and New York: Continuum, 2007.

Gabriel, George S. *Mary. The Untrodden Portal of God*. Ridgewood, NJ: Zephyr Publishing, 2nd ed., 2005.

[Maximovitch], Blessed Archbishop John. *The Orthodox Veneration of the Mother of God*. Platina, CA: St Herman of Alaska Brotherhood, 1987.

---

[6]These include, most recently, Tina Beattie, *God's Mother, Eve's Advocate* (London and New York: Continuum, 1999; rev. ed. 2002); Boss, ed., *Mary: The Complete Resource*; C. Maunder, ed., *The Origins of the Cult of the Virgin Mary* (London and New York: Burns and Oates, Continuum, 2008).

Pelikan, Jaroslav. *Mary Through the Centuries: Her Place in the History of Culture.* New Haven, CT and London: Yale University Press, 1996.

Schmemann, Alexander. *The Virgin Mary, Celebration of Faith*, vol. 3. Crestwood, NY: St Vladimir's Seminary Press, 2001.

chapter one

THE MOTHER OF JESUS CHRIST: THE VIRGIN MARY IN SCRIPTURE

Scripture is the basis for much Christian reflection on the Mother of God: it provides us both with a historical narrative and with theological interpretation of this narrative. Scripture, in Orthodox as well as all other Christian traditions, includes the Old and New Testaments. The latter could never have been written without the books that originally circulated as Hebrew Scripture. Every text that Christians wrote from the middle of the first century AD onward was informed usually in an inter-textual, or interwoven, way that expresses the unity of Scripture by the books belonging to the historical, prophetic, poetic, and wisdom traditions of the Old Testament.

As scholars have recently emphasized, Scripture is "the word of God in human words."[1] Orthodox Christian tradition interprets

[1] J. Breck, *Scripture in Tradition. The Bible and its Interpretation in the Orthodoxy Church* (Crestwood, NY: St Vladimir's Seminary Press, 2001), 9; quotation from T. Stylianopoulos, "Scripture and Tradition in the Church," in M.B. Cunningham and E. Theokritoff, eds., *The Cambridge Companion to Orthodox Christian Theology* (Cambridge: Cambridge University Press, 2008), 23.

Scripture with the help of the Patristic commentators and the liturgy, by the inspiration of the Holy Spirit. In other words, the Church is the guide for reading and understanding the biblical witness. The context in which Christians receive this guidance is most often in church services where Scripture is read aloud, interpreted by preachers, and woven into every text that is used in liturgical worship.

In this chapter, we will examine the biblical texts that began to circulate in the course of the first century in order to find out what they tell us about Mary, the mother of Jesus Christ. As we shall see, such sources were not intended to serve merely as historical narratives; they bore witness to divine revelation. The Evangelists saw the Virgin Mary as someone who had been destined by God to bear his Son, as the Old Testament prophets had foretold. Even in this earliest period in Christian history, writers thus attempted to hold the divinity and humanity of Christ in balance; this paradox was also manifested in the character and background of his mother. Mary, for such early writers, was already seen as the holy birth-giver of Christ, the Son and Word of God; at the same time, however, she was a young woman who was fully human, living out her life in first-century Palestine.

We will first explore the Old Testament witness to Mary, the Mother of God, since these historical and prophetic books provide the foundations for Christian interpretation of Christ's birth. After this, we shall move on to examine what New Testament texts say about the Virgin Mary. Whereas some books, such as the Pauline Epistles, are surprisingly reticent about the role of the Mother of God in Christ's life, the Gospels of Luke and John have more to say on the subject. The chief purpose of all of the New Testament writers was to bear witness to Christ's Incarnation, Passion, and Resurrection. The Mother of God played an important role, both physically and morally, in helping to bring the Son of God into the world, but the Evangelists did not portray her at the center of his ministry or Passion. This decision was reversed later, as we shall see in Chapter Two, by some apocryphal and medieval Christian writers, but freedom to interpret the biblical narrative in such a dynamic way was slow to develop. Finally, towards the end of this chapter, we shall look briefly at two other books in the New Testament, Acts and Revelation, for their treatment of the Mother of God. The combined witness of the texts that were eventually accepted into the biblical canon offers a picture of the Virgin that is not complete, as regards her background and character, but which helps Christians to understand who Jesus was and how his coming had been foretold.

The Old Testament

"Therefore the Lord himself will give you a sign. Look, the Virgin will conceive in her womb, and will bear a son, and you will call his name Emmanuel" (Is 7.14).[2] This is the most explicit prophetic reference to the Mother of God in the Old Testament and

[2]Translations of the Old Testament according to the Greek Septuagint version are based throughout this book on J. Allen and M. Najim, eds., *The Orthodox Study Bible* (St Athanasius Academy of Orthodox Theology. Nashville, Dallas, Mexico City, Rio de Janeiro and Beijing: Thomas Nelson, 2008) and A. Pietersma and B.G. Wright, eds., *A New English Translation of the Septuagint* (Oxford: Oxford University Press, 2007). In each case, the primary source, along with any modifications that I may have introduced, will be indicated in footnotes. Translations from the New Testament, following the guidelines of St Vladimir's Seminary Press, are taken from *The Holy Bible. Revised Standard Version* (New York: Thomas Nelson and Sons, 1953).

it contains the essential facts concerning the Incarnation of Christ. "Emmanuel," meaning, "God is with us" in Hebrew, refers to the Messiah; his mother, who will conceive him in her womb, will be a virgin ("parthenos"). The use of "parthenos" in the Greek Septuagint represents, arguably, an interpretation of the Hebrew "almah," which has the more general meaning of "young girl." Nevertheless, Christian writers, beginning with the Evangelist Luke, have always accepted this version of the text, along with its mysterious implications concerning the birth of Christ.

The prophecy in Micah 5.2–3 adds to the information provided by Isaiah. Here we learn that the birth will take place in a town in Judah called Bethlehem, that the One born will be "Ruler in Israel," and that this was planned eternally:

> And you, Bethlehem, house of Ephratha, are very few in number among the thousands of Judah; one from you will come forth for me to become a ruler of Israel; and his goings forth were from the beginning, even from eternity. Therefore he will grant them until the time when she who is in labor shall give birth . . .

The phrase, "she who is in labor," must refer to the "virgin" of Isaiah; her essential role in the advent of the Lord is indicated by this admonition to Israel to wait until her time has come. Most Patristic commentators have regarded this prophecy as echoing that in Isaiah 7.14, although modern scholars have occasionally offered alternate explanations such as that Micah is referring not to the virginal mother, but to the tribe Ephrath of Bethlehem, out of which the Messiah would come.[3]

---

[3]H. Graef, *Mary. A History of Doctrine and Devotion* (rev. ed. Notre Dame, IN: Ave Maria Press, 2009), 4.

Whereas Isaiah and Micah contain the most explicit prophecies concerning the birth of Christ from the Virgin Mary, many other passages in the Old Testament are believed by Christian (both Patristic and modern) commentators to refer to her. Some texts, such as the Psalms and the Song of Songs, obliquely offer praise to the one who both contained and gave birth to God. In Psalm 86 (87).5, for example, we read, "A man will say, 'Zion is my mother and a man was born in her; and the Highest himself has founded her,' " or in Psalm 109 (110).3, "I have begotten you from the womb before the morning-star." The Song of Songs offers many allusions to the Virgin's place both in creation and in the Incarnation, as, for example, in the lines, "As a lily among brambles, so is my companion among the daughters" (Song 2.2). Such poetic imagery is allusive rather than explicit and only Christian commentators would interpret this passage as a reference to the Virgin Mary. Nevertheless, such associations began to be made by Christian exegetes from a very early period. Poetic metaphor, especially in a biblical context, was seen as one of the most effective ways in which the mystery of Mary's role in the Incarnation of Christ might be expressed.

Typology, or the foreshadowing of the Christian dispensation in events, people, or places of the Old Testament, plays an important part in Orthodox reflection on the Mother of God. Typology is a method of scriptural interpretation that developed very early in Christian tradition. It is closely related to—or even perhaps a form of—allegorical exegesis in its revelation of the deeper links between the Old and New Testaments and of the divine plan that has been unfolding throughout human history. St John of Damascus describes Old Testament types as "images of the future" in his first treatise in defense of holy icons:

Again there are said to be images of the future, describing the things to come in shadowy enigmas, as the ark foreshadows the holy Virgin Mother of God, as does the rod and the jar; and the serpent the one who did away with the bite of the primordially evil serpent through the cross; or the sea, water, and the cloud the Spirit of baptism.[4]

As we see in this passage, such signs may refer not only to the Mother of God, but also to Christ or to the Christian sacraments. Archimandrite Ephrem Lash suggests that the Fathers identified Old Testament types in course of their prayer and meditation on Scripture.[5] They recognized the hidden, even secret, nature of such signs. Frances Young, inspired by studies of the fourth-century liturgical writer, St Ephrem the Syrian, emphasizes the way in which Old Testament types belong to sacred time: they lift the event, person, or object out of its historical context and reveal its eternal meaning.[6] Whereas this interpretation of the eternal meaning of typology is valuable, it is correct to emphasize, as John Breck does, the extent to which both types and antitypes also remain rooted in the historical narrative of the Christian dispensation. This method of biblical interpretation thus embodies, even more than allegory, a paradoxical juxtaposition of temporal and eternal meaning.

[4]John of Damascus, *Treatise* I.12, trans. A. Louth, *Three Treatises on the Divine Images* (Crestwood, NY: St Vladimir's Seminary Press, 2003), 27.

[5]Archimandrite Ephrem Lash, "Mary in Eastern Church Literature," in A. Stacpoole, OSB, ed., *Mary in Doctrine and Devotion* (Dublin: Columba Press, 1990), 58–80.

[6]Francis Young, *Biblical Exegesis and the Formation of Christian Culture* (Cambridge: Cambridge University Press, 2002), 152–7; Sebastian Brock, *The Luminous Eye. The Spiritual World Vision of Saint Ephrem the Syrian* (Kalamazoo, MI: Cistercian Publications, 1985), 29–30.

Typology also performs a metaphorical function in that it expresses a connection between the Mother of God and created objects or places. Biblical types that refer to Mary, the Mother of God, reveal different aspects of her mysterious role in the Incarnation. These include Jacob's ladder (Gen 28.10–17), the burning bush (Ex 3.1–8), the tabernacle and many of its furnishings (Ex 26, 35, 36 and 40), Gideon's fleece (Judg 6.27–40), and many others. In theological terms, such images express Mary's roots in creation: she is a human being, yet she also contains or transmits divinity in her conception and bearing of the incarnate Christ. Typology thus expresses in both a theological and poetic way the paradoxical mystery that lies at the heart of Christian doctrine.

Marian types are employed especially in the offices that make up the vigils for important feasts (with certain types being chosen for particular contexts, such as the temple and its furnishings for the feast of the Entry of the Mother of God into the temple).[7] Such types have formed a part of Orthodox tradition for so many centuries that Christian comprehension of their meaning is taken for granted. It is also worth emphasizing that typology represents a subtle form of teaching about truths that are ineffable. For Gregory of Nazianzus, the best theologian is the one who "assembles more of Truth's shadow."[8] Such signs not only foretell, but also embody, the mysterious role of Mary in the Incarnation of Christ. Just as the bush was engulfed in the flame of divine fire while remaining unconsumed (Ex 3.2), so did

[7]P. Ladouceur, "Old Testament Prefigurations of the Mother of God," *St Vladimir's Theological Quarterly* 50:1–2 (2006), 5–57.

[8]Gregory of Nazianzus, *Oration 30*, trans. F.M. Young, *God's Presence: A Contemporary Recapitulation of Early Christianity* (Cambridge: Cambridge University Press, 2013), 393.

Mary conceive and give birth to God while remaining a virgin. Gideon's fleece, as John Chrysostom reminds us, expresses the secret and self-effacing way in which Christ became incarnate.[9] The tabernacle, and later Solomon's temple, foreshadowed the way in which the Son of God himself would inhabit the Virgin Mary's womb. From about the fourth century onward, typology became the preferred way of teaching and meditating on Scripture in the Orthodox Church, especially with regard to the role of the Mother of God in the divine dispensation. This tendency is especially evident in the hymns and readings of the great Marian feasts of the Church.

Whether it is interpreted literally, morally, or allegorically (and Patristic and liturgical exegesis of Scripture is usually a combination of all three), the Old Testament continually points forward to the arrival in creation of Christ, the Savior, with the help of his mother, the Virgin Mary. Such testimony to God's redemptive plan for humanity, which bears witness both to the Mother of God and to Christ, represents the basis for all subsequent reflection on this divine and saving mystery.

The New Testament: the Epistles of St Paul

Turning to the New Testament, the authentic Epistles of St Paul, dated to around the fifties AD, are the earliest witnesses to the life and teachings of Christ. These short texts, which were written to guide individual Christian communities in Asia Minor, Greece, and Rome, reflect St Paul's mission to spread the new faith and

---

[9]John Chrysostom, *Commentary on the Psalms (Ps 49 [50]. 2)*, trans. R.C. Hill (Brookline, MA: Holy Cross Press, 1998), 1.352; quoted in Ladouceur, "Old Testament Prefigurations of the Mother of God," 25–6.

to safeguard its orthodoxy. In all of his letters, St Paul's central focus is Christ, that is, the risen Messiah, whose coming superseded the laws of the old dispensation and initiated the grace and life of the new. St Paul's lack of attention to Christ's mother, the Virgin Mary, is puzzling in view of the Old Testament prophecies and types that have just been cited. He refers specifically to Mary only once, in Galatians 4.4–5: "But when the time had fully come, God sent forth his Son, born of woman, born under the law, to redeem those who were under the law, so that we might receive adoption as sons." St Paul refers to prophecy here, which foretold that a young woman or virgin would, in the fullness of time, give birth to the Messiah. The phrase, "born under the law," serves to link the new dispensation with the old: whereas Mary, a mortal woman, bore Christ in accordance with the rules of the old dispensation and on behalf of the Jews who belonged to that order, this event heralded the beginning of a new dispensation in which all of humanity, including Jews and gentiles, would receive new birth.

This passage is brief, but also significant, in what it reveals about St Paul's understanding of the Virgin Mary's role in the Incarnation of Christ. Later Christian writers picked up on his portrayal of the Mother of God as the link between the old and the new dispensations, the eras of law and grace, prophecy and fulfillment. The Apostle was in fact the first Christian writer to explore how the old and new covenants are linked together in both historical and symbolic ways.[10]

---

[10]See also, for example, I Corinthians 10.4.

The Gospels: infancy narratives

Turning to the Gospels, it is only the Evangelists Matthew and Luke who recount the story of Christ's nativity. The latter, in his infancy narrative (Lk 1.26–38), focuses on Mary as the central character, providing some essential facts about this young Jewish virgin: She lives in Nazareth, a town in the northern part of Palestine, is engaged to a man called Joseph, and is named Mary. Besides this, however, the Evangelist emphasizes the Virgin's reaction to the extraordinary message of the archangel. She is "troubled" by his words, wondering what they mean. When Gabriel provides her with more details about the miraculous conception that is about to occur, Mary questions him further and asks, logically enough, how she, as a virgin, can possibly conceive a child.

Later Orthodox preachers and hymnographers loved to focus on Luke's portrayal of Mary and response to the archangel's greeting. In their re-telling of the story, they elaborated the dialogue in order to make this scene come to life for Christian congregations. St John of Damascus' kanon for the feast of the Annunciation, for example, contains a dramatic dialogue in which Gabriel and the Virgin Mary speak antiphonally in successive stanzas.[11] Such dialogues, like the Gospel account on which they are based, display the Virgin's human response to this miraculous event. She is frightened and even doubtful of the archangel's credentials; however, on hearing his message, she comes freely to believe and accept God's will. Luke again emphasizes Mary's thoughtful nature in the narrative that follows: After the shepherds have

[11] Mother Mary and Archimandrite Kallistos Ware, trans., *The Festal Menaion* (London and Boston: Faber and Faber, 1969), 448–58.

come to glorify the newborn child lying in the manger, he tells us that "Mary kept all these things, pondering them in her heart." (Lk 2.19). And twelve years later, when Jesus is found teaching Jewish teachers in the temple, the Evangelist writes again, "his mother kept all these things in her heart" (Lk 2.51).

Luke also employs Old Testament prophecy and typology in his telling of Christ's infancy narrative. This deeper meaning would not have been lost on the earliest Christians; it is also recognized by Orthodox worshippers today, largely because liturgical hymns help to remind them of these biblical references. Mary's song of praise, the "Magnificat," which she utters after visiting Elizabeth and receiving both her cousin's and the unborn John the Baptist's endorsement of her conception, recalls Hannah's prayer in 1 Kings 2.1–10 LXX (1 Sam 2.1–10) when the latter dedicates her young son Samuel, the future prophet, to the temple. The wording of the Magnificat, which begins, "My soul magnifies the Lord . . . ," is reminiscent of many other songs of praise in the Old Testament, especially those contained in the Psalms.[12] The Magnificat is an exuberant hymn of praise in which the Virgin, like other faithful worshippers before her, celebrates the greatness and mercy of her God; above all, she recalls his help to his chosen people from the earliest times.

Inter-textual biblical allusions may be conveyed even more subtly than this, however. When the archangel says to Mary, "The Holy Spirit will come upon you, and the power of the Most High will overshadow you . . ." (Lk 1.35), the language and imagery combine to recall God's creative activity at the very beginning of time, when "the Spirit of God was moving over <the face> of the waters."

---

[12]See, for example, Psalms 33 (34).3; 34 (35).27; 39 (40).16

(Gen 1.3).[13] As Sarah Jane Boss has remarked, Mary was a virgin in the same way that the universe was "without form and void" (Gen 1.2) at the beginning of time; nothing had yet been created in her. When she consented to God's will and conceived Christ, she recapitulated, or completed, the original creation: "Jesus is himself the new creation, in whom the universe is restored and fulfilled, and so it is only the language of God's creation of the universe that can do justice to the cosmic significance of Christ's conception."[14] Another Old Testament reference, which is conveyed in the word "overshadow" (Greek ἐπισκιάζω), is Exodus 40.35, after Moses' completion of the tabernacle in accordance with God's instructions, when "the cloud overshadowed it and the tabernacle was filled with the glory of God." Luke's choice of similar vocabulary to describe the mysterious process, involving both the Holy Spirit and the "power of the Most High," in the conception of Christ must be deliberate: like the tabernacle, a type that is commonly used to designate the Mother of God in Orthodox liturgical texts, Mary was filled with God's glory as he emptied himself and took on her physical nature.

The Evangelist Matthew focuses less explicitly on the Mother of God in his telling of the nativity story; nevertheless, she remains important in the narrative. Matthew tells us that Mary was found to be expecting a child "from (ἐκ) the Holy Spirit" when she was engaged to, but not yet living together with, Joseph. Joseph had resolved to dismiss her quietly from their marriage contract when an angel of the Lord appeared to him and told him that the child

---

[13]This translation is taken from A. Louth, ed., *Ancient Christian Commentary on Scripture, Old Testament I: Genesis 1–2* (Chicago and London: Fitzroy Dearborn Publishers, 2001), 4.

[14]S.J. Boss, *Mary* (London and New York: Continuum, 2003), 4.

had been conceived from the Holy Spirit. Citing prophecy (Is 7.14), Matthew informs us that this child would be named "Emmanuel," which may be translated, "God is with us." (Mt 1.20–23). In this version we see an emphasis on prophetic testimony: every event takes place in the manner that was foretold, including Herod's massacre of infants and Rachel's lament (Jer 31.15), the flight into Egypt, and Christ's eventual return to Palestine from there (Hos 11.1).[15]

Both Matthew and Luke thus endow their infancy narratives with prophetic and symbolic meaning that can be read at a number of levels. Christians today, like their first-century counterparts, cannot fail to recognize the theological significance of the conception and nativity of Christ. By alluding to earlier examples of God's immanence in creation and to his revelation of future salvation by the agency of the prophets, the Evangelists convey to their readers the significance of this Incarnation. Thus, theological considerations are equally, if not more, important than historical ones in their telling of the story. Given Mary's importance in the infancy narratives, it is surprising that the four Evangelists do not focus more on the personal holiness of the Mother of God elsewhere in their narratives. This silence, which has led some Protestants to question the honor paid to the Virgin Mary in the Roman Catholic and Orthodox Churches, does demand some investigation, even if a definitive answer is not possible.

---

[15]Hosea 11.1 reads, ". . . out of Egypt I called my Son." "The Son of God" in this context is Israel; in Matthew Christ is the new Israel. He recapitulates in his own life the history of Israel, without falling into sin.

Mary and the Ministry of Christ

Many modern scholars have commented on the fact that the Virgin Mary appears so infrequently in the sections of the Gospels that deal with Jesus Christ's adult role as teacher and Messiah.[16] Whereas Patristic writers pointed to the mystery that surrounds not only the Virgin Mary but also the Incarnation itself, more modern commentators have suggested, with equal plausibility, that the Evangelists are relatively silent about Mary in these sections of the Gospels because they are focusing on developments in the life of Christ. This is the period in which Jesus, as the Messiah whom most do not yet recognize as Son of God, collects a circle of disciples, teaches a growing number of followers, performs miracles, and in effect creates a new family, or community, that is based on faith. On one occasion, as we are told in the synoptic Gospels, Jesus appears to reprimand his mother and "brothers" (Mt 12.46–50, Mk 3.31–35, Lk 8.19–21). This episode, which might at first glance seem disrespectful of the Mother of God, gains meaning if its positive message is understood. Christ is emphasizing here the new, spiritual family of discipleship, as opposed to the family based on kinship ties. He then says, according to the Evangelist Matthew, ". . . whoever does the will of my Father in heaven is my brother and sister and mother" (Mt 12.50).[17] As in the case of a parallel passage in Luke 11.27–28, when Christ says, "Blessed indeed are those who hear the word of God and keep it!"

[16]See, for example, Pelikan, *Mary Through the Centuries*, 8; R.E. Brown, K.P. Donfried, J.A. Fitzmyer, J. Reumann, eds., *Mary in the New Testament* (New York and Mahwah, NJ: Paulist Press, 1978), 11–12.

[17]For this interpretation by an Orthodox commentator, see V. Lossky, *In the Image and Likeness of God*, ed. J.H. Erickson and T.E. Bird (Crestwood, NY: St Vladimir's Seminary Press, 2001), 197.

in response to a woman who reminds him of his mother's blessed-
ness, Orthodox tradition stresses the positive aspect of this statement: Mary is pre-eminently someone who obeyed God's word,
thereby becoming—even before he was born—Christ's first disciple. The passage is read out during the Divine Liturgy on most
of the Orthodox feasts that honor Mary, the Mother of God.[18]

Mary at the Cross and at the Tomb

Christian commentators have always been puzzled by the fact
that the Gospel accounts of the final events in Christ's life, leading
up to the Crucifixion and the Resurrection, are somewhat different. The four Evangelists agree in saying that most of the disciples
fled from the final sufferings of their Lord, but their descriptions
of the faithful women who stayed by the cross and of those who
brought myrrh to the tomb diverge in a number of ways.

To begin with the scene at the cross, Matthew and Mark both
state, after describing Christ's death and the upheaval in creation
that followed it, that women were there, watching from a distance. According to Matthew, these included Mary Magdalene,
Mary the mother of James and Joseph, and the mother of the
sons of Zebedee (Mt 27.55–56). Mark agrees by and large with
this account, except that he names the third woman as Salome
(Mk 15.40), while Luke simply calls them "the women who had
followed him from Galilee" (Lk 23.49), without referring to any

---

[18]See also the discussion of this passage in Brown, Donfried, Fitzmyer, and
Reumann, *Mary in the New Testament*, 170–72. For the liturgical readings, see Mother Mary and Archimandrite Kallistos Ware, trans., *The Festal
Menaion*, 130 (Nativity of the Mother of God), 197 (Entry into the Temple),
528 (Dormition of the Mother of God).

of them by name. The Gospel of John differs from the synoptic accounts in stating explicitly that Mary, the Mother of Jesus, was present, along with her sister, also named Mary and wife of Clopas, and Mary Magdalene (Jn 19.25). John also uniquely tells the story of Christ's last words to his mother and beloved disciple, who is usually presumed to be John himself: "When Jesus saw his mother and the disciple whom he loved standing near, he said to his mother, "Woman, behold your son." Then he said to the disciple, "Behold your mother." And from that hour the disciple took her to his own home." (Jn 19.26–27).

From as early as the second century, Christian theologians attempted to explain the discrepancies between the Gospel accounts. The most common solution for the different lists of women is to suggest that Mary, the mother of James and Joseph (or Joses), was the Mother of God herself: John Chrysostom, for example, writes, "But who were these? His mother, for she is called mother of James, and the rest."[19] Orthodox tradition maintains that Mary, the Mother of God, became mother to Joseph's children by a previous marriage; one of these was "the brother of the Lord," James.[20] Thus, if we accept, as did the Fathers, that Matthew and Mark named the Virgin, as did John, while Luke simply implied her presence among the women who had followed Jesus from Galilee, then the accounts, at least as far as she is concerned, are in harmony.

[19]John Chrysostom, *Homily 88 on Matthew*, trans. G. Prevost, in P. Schaff, ed., A Select Library of Nicene and Post-Nicene Fathers of the Christian Church (Edinburgh: T. & T. Clark; repr. Grand Rapids: Eerdmans, 1988–91) [hereafter NPNF]', First Series, vol. 10, 522.

[20]John McGuckin, *The Orthodox Church. An Introduction to its History, Doctrine and Spiritual Culture* (Oxford: Blackwell Publishing, 2008), 214.

Later liturgical writers, such as the sixth-century poet Romanos the Melodist, vividly portray the parting scene between Jesus and his mother as she stands at the foot of the cross. Romanos describes the Virgin weeping and protesting at this unjust death, while Christ attempts to explain its meaning and to reassure her:

As Mary from her deep grief
and great sorrow cried out thus and wept, he turned
to her, he that had come from her, and cried,
"Why are you weeping, Mother? Why are you carried
away like the other women?
Should I not suffer? Not die? How then shall I save Adam?
Should I not dwell in a tomb? How then shall I draw to
life those in hell?
And indeed, as you know, I am being crucified unjustly.
Why, then, do you weep, Mother? Rather shout out,
'Willingly he suffered, my Son and my God!'"[21]

Romanos does not focus on Christ's entrusting of his mother to his disciple John in this kontakion. Instead, he stresses Mary's maternal qualities, while also suggesting, by means of words that he imagines her Son might have spoken, that she is different from other women and must rise above her grief. In the next stanza, Christ says to her:

"Put away, then, Mother, put away your grief.
You should not lament, for you were named Full of Grace.

[21]Trans. Archimandrite Ephrem, *St Romanos, On the Life of Christ. Kontakia* (San Francisco, London and Pymble: HarperCollins, 1995), 144–5. 4; P. Maas and C.A. Trypanis, eds., *Sancti Romani Melodi Cantica. Cantica Genuina* (Oxford: Clarendon Press, 1963), 143.

Do not cover up your title with weeping.
Do not make yourself like those without understanding,
    all-wise Maiden.
You are at the heart of my bridal chamber.
Do not then, as though you stood outside, waste away
    your soul.
Address those in the bridal chamber as your slaves;
for everyone will come running with fear and will obey
    you, honored Lady,
when you say, 'Where is my Son and my God?' "[22]

Here we find a strong statement of Mary's theological importance and privileged status as the "bride" of Christ. She, of all people, should understand why Christ is on the cross; she is worthy of devotion and obedience from all Christians, as the Mother of God.

Turning to the scene at the tomb of Christ, we discover similar discrepancies in the Gospel accounts of the witness of the myrrh-bearing women. Here there is again some disagreement among the Evangelists about whether the Mother of God was among this small group of faithful women. According to Matthew, the myrrh-bearers included Mary Magdalene and "the other Mary" (Mt 28.1). Mark names Mary Magdalene, Mary the mother of James, and Salome as the myrrh-bearers, while Luke cites the same group, with the substitution of Joanna for Salome. Finally, and perhaps most oddly as far as later Christian commentators were concerned, John tells us that the only woman who came to the tomb was Mary Magdalene; she was also the first to behold

---

[22]Trans. Archim. Ephrem, *St Romanos, On the Life of Christ*, 145. 5; Maas and Trypanis, *Sancti Romani Melodi Cantica*, 143–4.

her risen Lord, when she mistook him at first for the gardener (Jn 20.1–18).

Mary Magdalene thus plays a prominent role in all four Gospel accounts. Apocryphal texts, such as the *Gospel of Mary*, emphasize her closeness to Christ even more emphatically, suggesting that she was the one disciple to whom he entrusted secret wisdom.[23] Orthodox Christian Fathers did not deny the importance of Mary Magdalene's role at the time of the Resurrection either, although some, such as St John Chrysostom, suggested that she acted as she did because, unlike the male disciples, she was both slow to understand the meaning of the Resurrection and prone to strong emotion. This, according to Chrysostom, explains why she remained weeping at the tomb while the men went home.[24] Some early Fathers also stress how appropriate it is that a woman was the first to see the risen Christ, since it was also a woman, Eve, who brought about the fall from grace.[25]

It is the Mother of God, however, who more usually assumes the title of "Second Eve," from as early as the second century. As we shall see in Chapter Three, this is based on a typology that relates specifically to Eve's acceptance of the devil's counsel in Genesis 3,

---

[23]This Gospel, which is generally labelled "gnostic", was originally written in Greek sometime in the second century. It survives in Coptic in the Nag Hammadi collection of texts; an English translation may be found in J.M. Robinson, ed., *The Nag Hammadi Library in English* (Leiden: Brill, 1996), 524–7.

[24]John Chrysostom, *Homily 86 on John*, trans. P. Schaff, NPNF, First Series, vol. 14, 323. See also Ammonios of Alexandria, *Explanation of the Gospel of John*, J.-P. Migne, ed., *Patrologia Graeca* (Paris, 1800–75) [hereafter "PG"] 85, 1516–21.

[25]See, for example, Gregory of Nazianzus, *Second Oration on Easter* 24, trans. C.G. Browne and J.E. Swallow, NPNF, Second Series, vol. 7, 432.

---

which was replicated—and undone—by the Virgin's consent to the Annunciation in Luke 1.38. It is thus interesting to note that some liturgical writers, from as early as the fourth century, were beginning to suggest that the Virgin, as Second Eve, was the first person to encounter the risen Christ. St Ephrem the Syrian, for example, in a hymn on the Crucifixion, writes:

> Three angels were seen at the tomb:
> these three announced that he was risen on the third day.
> Mary, who saw him, is the symbol of the Church
> which will be the first to recognize the signs of his Second
> Coming.[26]

Romanos the Melodist, in the same kontakion on the Mother of God's lament at the foot of the cross that we considered earlier, has Christ tell her that she will be privileged to see him first after the Resurrection:

> When he heard this, the One who knows all things
> before their birth answered Mary, "Courage, Mother,
> because you will see me first on my coming from the
> tombs.[27]

These two hymn-writers, belonging to the fourth and sixth centuries respectively, are engaged in dynamic interpretation of Scripture. This means that instead of adhering literally to the somewhat

[26]Trans. L. Gambero, *Mary and the Fathers of the Church. The Blessed Virgin Mary in Patristic Thought* (San Francisco, CA: Ignatius Press, 1999), 115. J. Behr also quotes this passage in *The Mystery of the Church*, 133, commenting not only on the image of Mary as the Church, but also on the "dynamic" interpretation of Scripture that this hymn represents.

[27]Trans. Archim. Ephrem, *St Romanos, On the Life of Christ*, 148.12; Maas and Trypanis, *Sancti Romani Melodi Cantica*, 146–7.

divergent stories contained in the Gospels, they have decided to adjust the narrative for theological reasons. As we have seen, this does not imply a complete departure from the texts of the four Gospels: Mark and Matthew, at least, state that "Mary, the mother of James" was among the myrrh-bearers who came to the tomb very early on the day of the Resurrection. The belief that this was indeed the Mother of God is clearly stated in a text that is read out in the Matins service for Easter Sunday, thus revealing the eventual acceptance of this interpretation of the Gospels in Orthodox tradition:

> The Resurrection was known first to the Mother of God, who was sitting, as St Matthew says, opposite the tomb with the Magdalene. But that there might be no doubt of the Resurrection, because of its appropriateness to his Mother, the Evangelists say, "He appeared first to Mary Magdalene." She also saw the Angel on the stone and leaning down again she saw the ones inside the grave, who proclaimed the Lord's Resurrection. "For, they said, he has risen. He is not here. See the place where they laid him." On hearing this she ran and came to the leaders of the Apostles, Peter and John, and brought them the good news of the Resurrection.[28]

According to liturgical tradition, then, it is the Mother of God who first understood the fact of the Resurrection, but Mary Magdalene who saw the risen Christ and reported her encounter to the other disciples. This solution reflects a harmonization of the Gospel accounts, but also a dynamic, theological interpretation

---

[28]This occurs in the *Synaxarion of the Menaion*, sung after the sixth ode of the kanon. See the translation by Archimandrite Ephrem at <www.anastasis. org.uk/pascha.htm>.

of the scene, allowing Mary, the Mother of God, to play an active role in it.

Acts: Mary and the Apostles

Orthodox Christian icons of the Ascension of Christ into heaven usually accord Mary, his mother, a central position in the composition.[29] In some icons, the disciples point towards the Virgin, while she extends her hands to them in a gesture of blessing. This iconography depicts the Mother of God in her symbolic role as the Church. Christ has left this world and the Holy Spirit has yet to be sent down; Mary, as the Church, will meanwhile offer a haven and guidance to the disciples, along with all other followers of Christ.

The biblical basis for the scene can be found in Acts, the book (attributed to the Evangelist Luke) that describes the earliest missions of the apostles in Jerusalem and later, under the leadership of St Paul, in other parts of the Roman empire. Its description of the disciples' actions on the Mount of Olives and afterwards in "the upper room" in Jerusalem is tantalizingly brief, as regards Mary's position in this company. She is not mentioned at all at the scene of the Ascension, but when they return to Jerusalem we are told that "[the disciples] with one accord devoted themselves to prayer and supplication, together with the women and Mary the mother of Jesus, and with his brothers" (Acts 1.14).

This brief passage scarcely supports the depiction of Mary as a figure of authority, or even as symbolic image of the Church, that

[29]L. Ouspensky and V. Lossky, *The Meaning of Icons* (Crestwood, NY: St Vladimir's Seminary Press, 1983), 194–99 (image on p. 195).

we find in the Orthodox liturgical and iconographical traditions. However, as we have seen with regard to other moments in the Gospel narrative, such as the Resurrection, a dynamic interpretation of Scripture began to occur at an early date. This interpretation was supported not only by Patristic commentaries but also, as we shall see in the next chapter, by non-canonical or "apocryphal" texts that came to be accepted as an inspired form of tradition. Much later, in the Middle Byzantine period (*c.* AD 600–1204), several *Lives* (in other words, hagiographies or holy biographies) of the Mother of God added further details to the biblical core of the story.[30] The icon for the feast of the Ascension thus reflects a rich tradition that has a biblical basis, but one that was also elaborated in the course of the early Christian and medieval centuries.

Revelation 12: The Woman, her Child, and the Dragon

The Book of Revelation, which scholars believe may have been composed in the late first century, during a period of persecution under the Roman emperor Domitian (AD 81–96), has always been treated carefully in Orthodox Christian tradition,[31] even though

---

[30]For a provocative discussion of these *Lives*, the earliest of which is attributed to the seventh-century theologian Maximos the Confessor, see S.J. Shoemaker, "The Virgin Mary in the Ministry of Jesus and the Early Church according to the Earliest Life of the Virgin," *Harvard Theological Review* 98, no. 4 (2005), 441–67.

[31]Revelation is the only New Testament book that is never read in the services of the Orthodox Church. There may be various reasons for this, none of which involve a lack of respect for this apostolic text. See J. Allen, M. Najim, J.N. Sparks, and T. Stylianopoulos, eds., *The Orthodox Study Bible* (Nashville, TN: Thomas Nelson Publishers, 1993), 589. For a study of Revelation by an Orthodox author, see C.G. Flegg, *An Introduction to Reading the Apocalypse* (Crestwood, NY: St Vladimir's Seminary Press, 1999).

it is attributed to the Evangelist John and therefore accepted as canonical. While Orthodox tradition respects the apocalyptic—even mystical—teaching of Revelation, it has not exerted the same influence, in theological or imaginative terms, in the East as it has in the West.

A symbolic image appears in the twelfth chapter of Revelation that has sometimes been interpreted as referring to the Mother of God. This is the sign that appeared in heaven of a woman "clothed with the sun, with the moon under her feet, and on her head a crown of twelve stars." (Rev 12.1). The writer goes on to say that, being with child, she gave birth in great pain. After this, another sign appeared in heaven, namely, a fiery, red dragon with seven heads, ten horns, and seven diadems on his heads. The dragon stood in front of the woman so that he might devour her child as soon as it was born, but the child, a son, was snatched away and taken to God and his throne. The woman meanwhile fled into the wilderness, where she had a place prepared for God, so that there she can be "nourished for one thousand two hundred and sixty days" (Rev 12.6).

Patristic interpretation of the woman "clothed with the sun" alternates between associating her with the Virgin Mary and with the Church.[32] As in the Old Testament, where Israel is frequently depicted as a woman in labor (cf. Is 26.17), the woman of Revelation struggles to give birth to the child, who represents the body of Christ or the people of God. One of the problems with this interpretation is of course the statement that the woman gave birth in great travail (Rev 12.2), since the Fathers understood Mary's virgin birth of Christ to have taken place without corruption or pain.

[32]See Graef, *Mary. A History of Doctrine and Devotion*, 27–31.

However, if the passage is understood as referring to the painful process of change in the human condition that was initiated by Christ's Incarnation, and in which the Mother of God played a part, then it begins to make sense. The "woman," according to this more allegorical interpretation, can then be understood both as the Virgin Mary and as the Christian Church. In historical terms, it is likely that the reference to the woman's sojourn in "the wilderness" refers to a period of persecution under pagan emperors at the end of the first century. As the author of Revelation makes clear, however, she would be kept safe in this place even as her child (Christ) "was caught up to God and to his throne" (Rev 12.5–6).

Conclusion

Scripture reveals God's eternal, saving dispensation for humankind, which is fulfilled in the mystery of Christ's Incarnation, Passion, and Resurrection. This revelation was foreshadowed in the Old Testament, but fulfilled in the New. It is mediated by human writers, including Moses, the Evangelists, and apostolic teachers including St Paul, and it is interpreted with the help of the Holy Spirit. The core of this revelation is Christ, the Word and Son of God: according to the Fathers, Christians can understand the meaning of Scripture only if they read it as members of the body of Christ, illumined by "the True Light, that enlightens every man . . ." (Jn 1.9).

If we approach the Scriptures with this understanding, it becomes clear that Mary, Virgin and Mother of God, is essential to the story of Christ's Incarnation. She is the "earth" or "matter" that will produce, once the "power of the Most High" has overshadowed her (Lk 1.35), a new Adam (Christ) and a new creation. By freely accepting Gabriel's message and consenting to God's will, Mary undoes Eve's primal sin of disobedience. She subsequently offers heartfelt praise to the Lord in her "Magnificat" (Lk 1.46–55), also expressing here a message of justice and equality. She weeps for her Son at the foot the cross, but also accepts the disciple John (and by implication all other Christians) as her son in Christ's place (Jn 19.25–27). According to Orthodox tradition, as we saw above, Mary was among the myrrh-bearing women and was, with Mary Magdalene, one of the first human beings to see the Risen Lord.

From the early centuries of the Church onward, Christian tradition has continued to reflect not only on these New Testament passages, but also on the prophecies and signs within the Old Testament that foretell the Virgin Mary's central role in the mystery of the Incarnation. She is both human and a virgin even after giving birth to Christ. As so many Patristic commentators and liturgical poets tell us, Mary thus represents a physical link, or locus, where the divine and created worlds meet. She, like John the Baptist, is also interpreted by Christian writers beginning with St Paul, as the mediator between the old and the new covenants; for this reason the Virgin Mary would be blessed by all generations from that time forth (Lk 1.48).

Further Reading:

Breck, John. *Scripture in Tradition. The Bible and its Interpretation in the Orthodox Church*. Crestwood, NY: St Vladimir's Seminary Press, 2001.

Brown, Raymond E., K.P. Donfried, J.A. Fitzmyer, and J. Reumann, eds. *Mary in the New Testament*. New York and Mahwah: Paulist Press, 1978.

Goppelt, Leonhard. *Typos. The Typological Interpretation of the Old Testament in the New*, trans. D.H. Madvig. Grand Rapids, MI: Wm B. Eerdmans Publishing Co., 1982.

Stylianopoulos, Theodore. *The New Testament: An Orthodox Perspective. Scripture, Tradition, Hermaneutics*. Brookline, MA: Holy Cross Orthodox Press, 1997.

Stylianopoulos, Theodore. "Scripture and Tradition in the Church," in M.B. Cunningham and E. Theokritoff, eds., *The Cambridge Companion to Orthodox Christian Theology*. Cambridge: Cambridge University Press, 2008, 21–34.

chapter two

DANCING AT THE ALTAR: THE APOCRYPHAL AND LITURGICAL TRADITIONS

The liturgical texts and iconography that accompany the great Marian feasts of the Orthodox Church, including her Nativity (September 8), Entry into the Temple (21 November), and Dormition or "Falling Asleep" (August 15), contain many details that do not appear in the Old or New Testaments. One of the most vivid of these, to which the title of this chapter alludes, is the image of Mary, aged three, "dancing with her feet" on the third step of the altar in front of the Jewish temple.[1] This incident is described in an apocryphal book, called the *Protevangelium of James*, which scholars date to the middle or end of the second century.[2] The *Protevangelium* covers many of the gaps in Mary's history that we noted in the previous chapter, including her conception, birth, and childhood in the

---

[1] This detail may refer typologically to David's dancing "before the Lord with all his might" in 2 Kingdoms (2 Samuel) 6.14.

[2] Translated in J.K. Elliott, ed., *The Apocryphal New Testament. A Collection of Apocryphal Christian Literature in an English Translation based on M.R. James* (Oxford: Clarendon Press, rev. ed. 1999), 57–67.

temple, before going on to describe her betrothal to Joseph, the annunciation and the birth of Christ. Later, from the end of the fifth century AD, texts concerning the Virgin Mary's death and Assumption into heaven began to circulate in Christian circles.[3] Once these, along with the *Protevangelium*, came to be accepted as authoritative—even if not canonical—sources, they began to influence the liturgical and somewhat later, the iconographical traditions of the Orthodox Churches.

In this chapter we will explore the background and content of these apocryphal texts, their influence on liturgy, and finally the way in which they enriched Orthodox perceptions of the Mother of God. In the course of this discussion, we shall also consider some other textual influences on the Byzantine Marian tradition, including a set of *Lives*, or hagiographies, of the Mother of God that were written between the seventh and the tenth centuries. Fundamental to Orthodox acceptance of apocryphal or hagiographical material is the Scripture on which they are based; even if some texts were never believed to have apostolic origins, they were judged to be consistent, both in content and style, with biblical revelation. It is this quality, more than any basis in history, which caused some non-canonical texts to become so influential in the Orthodox liturgical tradition.

The *Protevangelium of James*

The "proto"-Gospel (thus named by modern scholars because it covers "the first" period before the birth of Christ) is attributed to St James, brother of the Lord, but was considered by

[3]S. Shoemaker, *Ancient Traditions of the Virgin Mary's Dormition and Assumption* (Oxford: Oxford University Press, 2002), 32, 38.

most early Fathers to be inauthentic. In other words, they took it seriously as an early Christian writing, but did not believe it to be the work of an early apostle. It rapidly became popular and was translated into many languages, including Syriac, Ethiopic, Georgian, Sahidic, Armenian, and probably Latin. Centuries later, versions also appeared in Old Church Slavonic and other medieval languages.[4] The early third-century theologians Clement of Alexandria and Origen both knew of the text and it continued to be cited by Fathers including Gregory of Nyssa and Epiphanius of Salamis. Nevertheless, it is interesting to note that before about the eighth century, Patristic writers were reluctant to cite the text by name, even if they did allude to its narrative in their treatises and sermons. After the eighth century, for reasons that will be discussed later, preachers including John of Damascus and Andrew of Crete drew freely on the *Protevangelium* as they taught their congregations about the Virgin Mary's conception, infancy and dedication to the temple. It was thus in the period between *ca.* AD 700 and 1000 that this text became so important in liturgical tradition, influencing not only the texts (both homilies and hymns) that adorned the newly established feasts of the Mother of God, but also the icons that were associated with them.

What then is the narrative content of this important apocryphal text? The *Protevangelium* begins with the Virgin Mary's parents, Saints Joachim and Anna, whom it describes as being wealthy and righteous but as lacking a child. The author of the text knows how significant the stigma would have been for sterile couples in the Jewish community of this period: Joachim, on bringing his gifts to the temple on the Day of Atonement, is rejected and goes into the

[4]Elliott, *The Apocryphal New Testament,* 52–55.

wilderness to grieve and pray to God. Anna, his wife, goes into her garden and also prays, singing a mournful lament to herself. Both figures are then granted a vision of angels, in which they are told that they will conceive a child who will attain great fame. Joachim returns home and embraces Anna at the gate; nine months later a daughter is born and named Mary. The *Protevangelium* goes on to describe how the baby is kept safe in Anna's chamber, without even being allowed to put her feet on the ground after she has taken her first seven steps, before being taken at the age of three to be dedicated to the Jewish temple. Here, after her joyful entrance when she dances on the steps of the altar, Mary is raised in the temple, being "nurtured like a dove" and fed by the hand of an angel. When she reaches the age of twelve and is no longer able to remain in these holy surroundings, the Virgin is betrothed to Joseph, an old man who has sons by a previous marriage. After being taken to his home "as his ward," Mary spins scarlet and purple threads for the temple curtain and encounters the Archangel Gabriel when drawing water at the well. After this event, the *Protevangelium* proceeds with the story of the Virgin's pregnancy and the birth of Christ, basing itself on the Gospels of Matthew and Luke. In the course of this narrative, the text emphasizes especially the virginal nature of this birth, introducing a midwife, named Salome, who conducts a physical examination in order to confirm that Mary has remained intact. There are echoes of other biblical and apocryphal stories here, such as Thomas's insistence on touching Christ's side after the resurrection (Jn 20.24–29) and a Jew's handling of the Virgin Mary's bier after her Dormition or "falling asleep," according to the apocryphal narratives concerning this event. In the *Protevangelium of James*, Salome is punished for her doubting attitude by the loss of her hand; it is restored only when she expresses her faith in Christ. The text concludes after describing the return of the magi to Persia and Herod's execution of Zacharias, who has hidden his son, John the Baptist, from the Jewish king.

It is clear that this early apocryphal text contains many elements in the Virgin Mary's story that do not appear in the canonical Gospels. This is not to say, however, that the *Protevangelium* disregards Scripture altogether. Both J.K. Elliott and Andrew Louth describe the text as a form of *midrash*, or commentary on the Bible;[5] this theory is persuasive since, at least in the sections that correspond to the Gospels, the narrative elaborates elements of the story that are treated only briefly in the original sources. Louth further suggests that the narrative exegesis of Scripture found in the *Protevangelium* is characterized above all by its emphasis on typology.[6] This can be illustrated by two examples taken from the narrative concerning Mary's childhood and preparation for her role as mother of Christ. In the first of these, Joachim calls for "undefiled daughters of the Hebrews" to accompany the child when she is brought to the temple at the age of three. This recalls Psalm 44 (45): 14–15 in which virgins accompany the royal daughter as she approaches the palace of the king, her spouse. Later liturgical writers would focus on this typological connection, emphasizing its bridal imagery in relation to the Virgin Mary and Christ. In our second example, Mary's spinning and weaving of the cloth for the temple is typologically prefigured by the veil

[5] Elliott, *The Apocryphal New Testament*, 48; A. Louth, "John of Damascus and the Mother of God as Link between Humanity and God," in L. Brubaker and M.B. Cunningham, eds., *The Cult of the Mother of God in Byzantium. Texts and Images* (Aldershot: Ashgate, 2011), 154–6.

[6] Louth, "John of Damascus and the Mother of God," esp. 156.

of Solomon's temple (2 Chronicles 3.14), but also foreshadows its tearing apart at the moment when Christ dies on the cross (Mt 27.51; Mk 15.38; Lk 23.45). At an even deeper level, the author may intend us to compare the weaving of the temple veil with the formation of Christ's body in Mary's womb. As Proclus of Constantinople would preach at the beginning of the fifth century, the Virgin became ". . . an awesome loom of the divine economy upon which the robe of union was ineffably woven."[7] Such symbolism is multi-layered, with many meanings revealing themselves to readers who understand the Christological meaning of the Old and New Testaments.

Scholars continue to debate why the *Protevangelium of James* was written and to puzzle over the reasons for its mixed reception by Christians in subsequent centuries. Some have suggested that the work was written for polemical reasons in order to refute rumors that were circulating in this period about the legitimacy of Christ's birth and the credentials of his mother Mary.[8] While apologetics may have played some part in the composition of the *Protevangelium*, it is even more likely that it reflects second-century Christians' growing preoccupation with Christ's conception and birth in the light of his divine nature as Word of God. Thus, whereas the *Protevangelium* seems, at first glance, to focus primarily on Christ's mother, the Virgin Mary, it is probably inspired as much by Christological considerations as by interest in her as a holy person. Mary's miraculous conception, protection in her infancy, and rearing in the temple underline her forthcoming role

---

[7]N. Constas, ed. and trans., *Proclus of Constantinople and the Cult of the Virgin in Late Antiquity. Homilies 1–5, Texts and Translations* (Leiden and Boston: Brill, 2003), 137.

[8]Elliott, *The Apocryphal New Testament*, 50.

as the container of the Divine Son. She, like the holy of holies, or innermost sanctuary in the temple, will become one of the few created locations that God chooses to inhabit. The physical reality of Christ's virgin birth, as emphasized in the *Protevangelium*, also bears witness to the fact that God has entered creation in a miraculous way, without causing any impurity to his mother in terms of Jewish tradition. Although the *Protevangelium* came later to be viewed as an important foundation of Christian devotion to the Mother of God, it should thus be read in its second-century context primarily as an exegetical text that elaborates on the infancy Gospels of Matthew and Luke.

Before leaving this important text and turning to the accounts of the Virgin's Dormition and Assumption into heaven, which were first written down several centuries later, we should briefly return to the reception of the *Protevangelium* by Christian thinkers after its appearance in the middle or end of the second century. The text is mentioned, as we saw above, by Clement of Alexandria and Origen at the beginning of the third century, and it continued to be cited occasionally by Greek Fathers of the fourth and fifth centuries. However, it is noticeable that writers such as Gregory of Nyssa, even when drawing on the *Protevangelium* for information about Mary's birth and childhood, avoid mentioning it by name. In his homily on the Nativity of Christ, Gregory reveals his knowledge of the Virgin's parents, their sterility and her dedication to the temple, but cites his source merely as "a certain apocryphal account."[9] After such reticence on the part of the early Fathers, it is therefore surprising to find eighth-century preachers such as John of Damascus embracing the *Protevangelium* as a source of information and theological inspiration concerning the

[9]PG 46, col. 1137D.

Theotokos. It is likely that this change in attitude had to do with the introduction of Marian feast-days in the liturgical calendar between the middle of the sixth and beginning of the eighth centuries. If Mary's Conception, Nativity, Entry into the Temple, and Dormition were to be formally celebrated in the Church, then the apocryphal texts should be openly acknowledged. It is also likely, as such texts were studied and assimilated into the liturgical tradition, that Byzantine theologians began to recognize their consistency with the biblical sources on which they were based, in terms of history, prophecy, and typology.

Accounts of the Virgin Mary's Dormition and Assumption into Heaven

The topic of the Virgin Mary's Dormition and Assumption into heaven has attracted considerable attention in recent years, especially from Roman Catholic scholars who have been eager to trace the textual foundations of the dogma that was formally endorsed by the Pope in 1950.[10] More recently, Stephen Shoemaker has identified various legends concerning the end of Mary's earthly life that emerged in the Syriac, Coptic, and Greek traditions towards the end of the fifth century.[11] It is likely that some uncertainty about the Virgin Mary's final days existed before this period. Epiphanius of Salamis, writing towards the end of the fourth century, states that he is unaware whether she died

[10]For extracts of Pope Pius XII's *Munificentissimus Deus*, see S.J. Boss, ed., *Mary: The Complete Resource* (London and New York: Continuum, 2007), 281–83.

[11]Shoemaker, *Ancient Traditions of the Virgin Mary's Dormition and Assumption.*

naturally or endured a martyr's death.[12] Once the narratives about the Dormition begin to appear, about a century later, they take various forms, which Shoemaker has convincingly grouped into separate families on the basis of their narrative content. One of these versions, which Shoemaker calls the "Palm of the Tree of Life" tradition, describes how Mary was approached and warned by an angel of her approaching death as she prayed on the Mount of Olives. This version influenced the first Greek homily on the Dormition, written by John of Thessalonica between 610 and 649, as well as later Byzantine liturgical texts on the subject.[13]

Although it varies slightly in the hands of different writers, the story can be summarized briefly, as follows: the Virgin Mary, as we have just seen, is accosted by an angel and given a palm from the Tree of Life as she prays on the Mount of Olives. She then returns home, calls together her friends and family, and announces the news to them. The apostles, who have spread throughout the inhabited world on their missions, are now miraculously transported in clouds to Mary's bedside. As she prepares herself for death, Christ arrives in a company of angels. He receives her soul and hands it to the Archangel Michael. The apostles then carry the Virgin's body on a bier to the tomb that has been prepared near the Garden of Gethsemane at the foot of the Mount of Olives. It is at this point in the narrative that an event that is frequently depicted in later icons of the Dormition occurs. A Jew, named Jephonias, lays hands on the funeral bier in order to upset it. An

[12]Epiphanius, *Panarion* 78.11.

[13]For an excellent introduction to these texts, along with translations of homilies by John of Thessalonica and other Byzantine preachers, see B.E. Daley, S.J., *On the Dormition of Mary. Early Patristic Homilies* (Crestwood, NY: St Vladimir's Seminary Press, 1998).

angel then punishes him by cutting off his hands, but Jephonias repents, prays to the Virgin, and is healed. Finally, the body is placed in the tomb. After three days, the tomb is found to be empty. The Virgin Mary's body has been assumed into heaven. Although some early texts might seem to imply the Virgin Mary's resurrection, pre-empting the process that will take place at the Final Day for all other human beings, it is noticeable that others, including many eighth- and ninth-century homilies on the Dormition, are more circumspect in their treatment of the issue. Brian Daley has suggested that preachers such as Andrew of Crete and John of Damascus were concerned to express the mystery that surrounds these events.[14] They saw Mary's death, as well as her Assumption into heaven, as ineffable and extraordinary; this is the glorious end of a person who has been fully deified in her role as holy Virgin and Birth-giver of God.

The Marian Feast-Days and their Liturgical Texts

The addition into the liturgical calendar of feast-days honoring events in the life of the Mother of God occurred slowly, between approximately the early sixth and eighth centuries. Just one Marian festival existed in the fifth century, celebrated on August 15 in Palestine but on December 26 in Syria and in Constantinople. The emperor Justinian, who came to power in the sixth century, added several more feasts to the calendar, including the Annunciation (March 25), the Presentation of Christ in the Temple (February 2), which gradually came also to commemorate the Virgin's Purification—and possibly her Nativity (September 8). According to the fourteenth-century historian Nikephoros Kallistos Xanthopoulos, it was the emperor Maurice (AD 582–602)

[14]Daley, *On the Dormition of Mary*, 27–28.

who instituted the feast of the Dormition in Constantinople on August 15. Finally, the feasts of St Anna's Conception of Mary (December 9) and the Virgin's Entry into the Temple (November 21) began to be attested in liturgical texts of the first half of the eighth century.[15]

Many of these new feasts, as we can see from their content, are based primarily—or even entirely—on apocryphal narratives. Those that celebrate Mary's Conception, Nativity and Entry into the Temple follow the account provided in the second-century *Protevangelium of James*. The Feast of the Dormition is based on post-fifth-century narratives of her death and Assumption into heaven. As we saw earlier, especially in connection with the *Protevangelium*, all of these non-canonical narratives build on scriptural foundations. The *Protevangelium* tells the same story of Christ's infancy, filling in gaps in Matthew's and Luke's narratives and also providing a detailed account of his mother's family background, birth, and education in the temple. Accounts of Mary's Dormition and Assumption go well beyond the canonical Scriptures in describing her final days, but they also adopt a narrative and style that is consistent with New Testament writings, building especially on what Luke says about the Virgin Mary in the first chapter of Acts. It is unlikely that these texts would have been accepted into the Byzantine liturgical tradition if they had been judged inconsistent with biblical revelation. There was, as we have seen, some reluctance in the first five centuries to cite them explicitly (although the Fathers did sometimes refer to them in their writings); however, with the introduction of new Marian

[15]See M.B. Cunningham, *Wider Than Heaven. Eighth-Century Homilies on the Mother of God* (Crestwood, NY: St Vladimir's Seminary Press, 2008), 19–28.

feast-days into the liturgical calendar from the early sixth century onward, liturgical writers began to employ these apocryphal texts openly in their homilies and hymns.

In the discussion that follows, we will focus on just two feasts, those of Mary's Entry into the Temple and her Dormition, in order to show how liturgical writers employed apocryphal sources in their compositions in honor of these subjects. Let us begin with the earliest homilies on the feast of the Entry into the Temple, which were written in the first half of the eighth century. It is noticeable first that the narrative found in the *Protevangelium of James* provides the preacher with a basic structure for his sermon. Germanus of Constantinople, writing in the early eighth century, describes how the three-year-old Mary was brought to the temple and entrusted to the care of the aged priest, whom he names as Zacharias (father of St John the Baptist), before being raised in the "holy of holies," the innermost sanctuary of the temple. The preacher invents a dialogue that might have taken place between the Virgin's mother Anna and the priest, in order both to add dramatic immediacy to the scene but also to explore their individual responses to this extraordinary event. Germanus is as interested in St Anna's feelings as he is in those of the elderly priest. He ascribes words to this holy figure in which she describes the range of emotions that she has experienced since learning of her conception and giving birth to Mary: she has felt desolation and loneliness, followed by inexpressible joy. Zacharias responds with exclamations of wonder and joy, recognizing the child as "the fulfillment of prophecy," "the seal of [God's] covenant," "manifestation of his mysteries," and many other laudatory epithets. The homily then goes on to describe the Virgin's sojourn in the temple, followed by her betrothal to

Joseph at the age of twelve.[16] This is a dramatic oration, which builds on the narrative provided in the *Protevangelium of James* and allows the congregation to consider both its human and divine implications.

Typological interpretation of the text is also important to Germanus, however, just as it would be to all subsequent liturgical writers on this theme. The central theme that we notice here is that the Virgin Mary is, by means of her stay in the Jewish temple, being prepared for her role as the living temple of the Lord. The preacher states in one passage, "Let us see how the all-holy one is today brought by her parents into the temple of God with the help of his priests, how the living temple of the Lord is taken up into the lifeless one . . ."[17] These lines express quite succinctly the transition that is taking place, as the old covenant gives way to, and is fulfilled in, the new. The event has been prophesied and God will soon enter his creation in an entirely new way: he will enter a living temple rather than the lifeless one that has lost its purpose. Hymns on the Entry of the Mother of God into the temple also stress this typological link, as we see in the following kontakion that is sung in Matins:

> The all-pure Temple of the Saviour, the precious Bridal Chamber and Virgin, the sacred treasure of the glory of God, is led today into the house of the Lord, and with her she brings the grace of the Holy Spirit. Of her God's angels sing in praise: "She is indeed the heavenly Tabernacle."[18]

[16]The homily is translated in Cunningham, *Wider Than Heaven*, 163–72.

[17]Cunningham, trans., *Wider Than Heaven*, 165.3.

[18]Mother Mary and Archimandrite Kallistos Ware, trans., *The Festal Menaion* (London: Faber and Faber, 1969; repr. S. Canaan, PA: St Tikhon's Seminary Press, 1998), 185.

This hymn reveals another strand of typological imagery, namely the concept of the Theotokos as Bride of Christ who is entering the bedchamber of her Lord to be united with him in body and spirit. In another sermon that is attributed to Germanus, the preacher uses similar imagery, quoting Psalm 44 (45) and the Song of Solomon in order to evoke Mary's bridal role. Here again he emphasizes the way in which the old order is giving way to the new, as the person in whom Christ will become incarnate is prepared.[19]

Such typological messages should not allow us to forget that the liturgical texts composed for the feast of the Entry of the Mother of God into the Temple also emphasize her human qualities, as a girl who is introduced into a holy place at a very young age. Gregory Palamas, preaching six centuries after Germanus, reminds us how Mary experienced nine years of *hesychia*, or stillness, during her stay in the temple. He emphasizes the fact that Mary is depicted both in the Gospels and in the *Protevangelium* as "one who listens"; not only did she listen to the Word of God at the Annunciation (Lk 1.38), but she "kept all these sayings, pondering them in her heart" (Lk 2.19, 51).[20] All of these meanings—prophetic, typological, and moral—are conveyed in the liturgical texts for this important feast. Church tradition has gathered them

---

[19]Cunningham, trans., *Wider Than Heaven*, 146. 1–2.

[20]Gregory Palamas, Homily 53, *On the Entry of the Theotokos into the Holy of Holies* II.52, trans. C. Veniamin, *Gregory Palamas, The Homilies* (Waymart, PA: Mount Thabor Publishing, 2009), 437–38; cited in Rt Revd Kallistos of Diokleia, "The Feast of Mary's Silence: The Entry into the Temple (21 Nov.)," in A. Stacpoole, ed., *Mary in Doctrine and Devotion. Papers of the Liverpool Congress, 1989, of the Ecumenical Society of the Blessed Virgin Mary* (Blackrock, Dublin: Columba Press, 1990), 34–41.

into a unified message of hope, fulfillment and awe in the face of a mystery that is best expressed by means of symbolic imagery.

The feast of the Dormition, which is informed by apocryphal texts that began to circulate in written form towards the end of the fifth century, as we have seen, also emphasizes the fulfillment of prophecy in its liturgical sermons and hymns. The eighth-century preacher and theologian, John of Damascus, opens his first in a trilogy of sermons for this feast with a passage that sums up the part that Mary has played in God's whole dispensation:

> For she was chosen from generations of old by the providential will and pleasure of God the Father, who begot you outside of time without alteration and without passion; she gave you birth, made flesh from herself at the end of the ages, to be our propitiation and salvation, our righteousness and our redemption—you who are "life from life and light from light, true God from true God."[21]

John, like other preachers of his day such as Andrew of Crete and Germanus of Constantinople, stresses especially the mysterious and awe-inspiring nature of the Virgin's Assumption into heaven. The event is testimony to Mary's glory as a human being who has attained true purity and sanctification in the course of her life; whereas her death was natural, she has been raised into heaven whence she acts as mediator and protector for the rest of humanity.

Hymns for the feast of the Dormition of the Mother of God emphasize the fact that the disciples, who were miraculously gathered together before her death, witnessed these events. They

[21]Daley, trans., *On the Dormition of Mary*, 185.3.

were filled with awe, but perceived the glory that had been conferred on Christ's mother. Mary's role as tabernacle or temple,
or in other words, as container of the Son of God himself, again
features prominently in the hymnography for this feast. But she
is also addressed as "ladder," "gate," "throne," along with other
epithets (which are also Old Testament types) that convey her
essential role in the Incarnation of Christ. As in the case of the
other Marian feasts, narrative, taken mainly from apocryphal
sources, combined with Old Testament typology and prophecy,
draws Orthodox congregations into active participation in the
event that is being celebrated in liturgical time. This synthesis
of both Scripture and apocryphal tradition was achieved largely
in the eighth and ninth centuries, when the Marian feasts had
begun to be celebrated universally and when a particularly creative group of hymnographers and preachers were at work in
Palestine and in Constantinople.

Byzantine *Lives* of the Mother of God

Before concluding this chapter on apocryphal or non-canonical
narratives on the Virgin Mary, it is worth looking briefly at a
remarkable set of texts that were written in Constantinople, possibly between the beginning of the seventh and before the end
of the tenth century. These can be described as hagiographical
since their purpose is apparently to provide new and comprehensive narratives about the Mother of God. As Stephen Shoemaker
has recently noted in relation to what is probably the earliest of
these, a *Life of the Virgin* that is attributed to the seventh-century
theologian Maximus the Confessor,[22] the extent to which they

[22]An English translation can be found in S. Shoemaker, *The Life of the
Virgin. Maximus the Confessor* (New Haven, CT: Yale University Press,

sometimes diverge from both biblical and apocryphal sources is striking.[23] This *Life*, for example, places Mary at the center of Christ's ministry, in charge of a group of female disciples who followed the Lord as he taught and worked miracles. Diverging again from the synoptic accounts, as well as from the Gospel of John, the *Life* describes the Mother of God standing outside the door when Christ was being interrogated, procuring the tomb for his burial, and keeping vigil there throughout the night. The author then tells us that Mary became leader of the disciples after Christ's resurrection; she took an active role in directing both their spiritual lives and missions. This narrative diverges in striking ways from those presented in the four Gospels and in the apocryphal texts that had been accepted into the Byzantine liturgical tradition. However, it circulated in monasteries from Mt Athos to Palestine and Sinai, according to the surviving manuscripts that transmit the text in its Georgian version.[24]

Three other *Lives* of the Mother of God survive from the Middle Byzantine period. They are attributed to an early ninth-century monk called Epiphanius, who probably lived at the Kallistratou Monastery in Constantinople, and to the tenth-century writers,

2012). Although Shoemaker places the original version of this text, which survives only in Georgian, in the early seventh century (suggesting even that it might have been written by Maximus), Phil Booth argues for a date several centuries later in his "On the *Life of the Virgin* attributed to Maximus the Confessor," *Journal of Theological Studies*, n.s. 66, Part 1 (2015), 149–203.

[23]See his discussion of the *Life* in S.J. Shoemaker, "The Virgin Mary in the Ministry of Jesus and the Early Church according to the Earliest *Life* of the Virgin," *Harvard Theological Review* 98:4 (2005), 441–67.

[24]Shoemaker, "The Virgin Mary in the Ministry of Jesus," esp. 441–2, 466–7.

Symeon Metaphrastes and John Geometres.[25] All of these texts, along with that attributed to Maximus the Confessor, share certain narrative features although they differ in some details in their telling of Mary's biography. It is notable that they all draw on both canonical and apocryphal accounts for inspiration. Reference to Old Testament prophecy and signs also pervades the narratives. The authors employ a method of exegesis that is both inter-textual and typological—in other words, they continually draw together passages and ideas from both the Old and New Testaments. However, it is the freedom with which these writers treat the Christological and Marian narratives that is most noticeable in this group of texts. Epiphanius, suggesting that the apocryphal sources are unreliable, states that he intends to provide his readers or hearers with a "true" account of the life of the Theotokos. He refers to a few Patristic sources, including writings by Eusebius of Caesarea, pseudo-Dionysius the Areopagite, John of Thessalonica, and Andrew of Crete, but diverges in significant ways even from these.

It is difficult to arrive at firm conclusions with regard to these middle Byzantine *Lives* of the Theotokos. What can be stated, on the basis of the surviving manuscripts, is that they do not

[25]None of these texts are easy to find since they are published in rare editions or have not yet been translated into English, or both. Epiphanius of Kallistratou's *Life* is edited in A. Dressel, ed., *Epiphanii monachi et presbyteri edita et inedita* (Paris-Leipzig, 1843), 13–44, following an earlier version that is printed in PG 120, 186–216. The Metaphrastic *Life* is published in B. Latysev, *Menologii anonymi byzantini saeculi* X (Petropolis [=St Petersburg], 1912), vol. 2, and that of John Geometres remains unedited, except for its final section which is published in A. Wenger, *L'assomption de la très sainte Vierge dans la tradition Byzantine du VIe au Xe siècle* (Paris, 1955), 364–415. I have consulted one of the surviving manuscripts, Cod. Vat. Gr. 504, fols. 173v–194v, in my recent study of the text.

appear to have circulated very widely, and that they did not exert much influence on liturgical or doctrinal sources. The message contained in Maximus' *Life of the Virgin* is certainly not typical of the more mainstream reflection that we have discussed elsewhere in this chapter. They remain odd features of a Byzantine literary culture that was perhaps not as unified as it sometimes appears. They are worthy of careful study, but evidently diverged too much from the New Testament and apocryphal narratives to be accepted fully into the Orthodox liturgical tradition.

Conclusions

This chapter has focused on various texts, most of which are usually described as "apocryphal," that gradually came to be accepted as authoritative in the Byzantine liturgical tradition. The earliest of these texts is the *Protevangelium of James*, written in the middle or at the end of the second century, while those on the Virgin Mary's Dormition and Assumption into heaven began to circulate after the end of the fifth century. These literary attempts to fill in details in Mary's story that are not provided in the canonical Gospels should be read as theological reflections on her mysterious role in the Incarnation of Christ. Like the canonical Gospels and Acts, they draw on Old Testament prophecy and typology for inspiration, weaving these together with oral testimony in order to provide theological justification for the part that Mary played in God's dispensation. An entirely literal reading of such symbolic accounts is problematic: even their authors would probably have admitted that some details, such as a three-year-old female child being admitted into the innermost sanctuary of the Jewish temple, are unlikely from a historical point of view. Much more important for the writers of such texts was the portrayal in evocative language of a mystery that was beyond understanding. Mary would soon become the holy place that God would inhabit; her preparation for this role needed therefore to be situated in a location that was symbolic of her own purity and holiness.

The apocryphal texts thus form part of the biblical *tradition* even if the Church never accepted them as belonging to the first rank of canonical, or apostolic, texts. They testified to authentic Christian revelation because they, like the liturgical texts were based on them, were faithful to a method of exegesis that had been adopted by the earliest Christian writers. It was, above all, the canonical Scripture, including both the Old and New Testaments, that informed the language and imagery of liturgical worship. These texts could, however, be augmented with the vivid—and still very biblical—details supplied by non-canonical texts.

Further Reading:

Cunningham, Mary B. *Wider Than Heaven: Eighth-Century Homilies on the Mother of God.* Crestwood, NY: St Vladimir's Seminary Press, 2008.

Daley, Brian E., trans. *On the Dormition of Mary. Early Patristic Homilies.* St Vladimir's Seminary Press, 1998.

Elliott, J.K., ed. *The Apocryphal New Testament. A Collection of Apocryphal Christian Literature in an English Translation based on M.R. James.* Oxford: Clarendon Press, rev. ed. 1999.

Shoemaker, Stephen J. *Ancient Traditions of the Virgin Mary's Dormition and Assumption.* Oxford: Oxford University Press, 2002.

Shoemaker, Stephen J., trans. *The Life of the Virgin. Maximus the Confessor.* New Haven, CT: Yale University Press, 2012.

chapter three
THE SECOND EVE AND MOTHER OF LIFE

One of the first prefigurations, or types, of Mary, the Mother of God, is Eve, whom God created as Adam's partner and helper in the Garden of Eden (Gen 2.21–25). Second-century Christian writers, including especially Irenaeus of Lyons, were the first to emphasize parallels between Eve and Mary: whereas the former chose to disobey God, the latter obeyed his word. Further, whereas Eve helped to bring about humanity's fall from grace, introducing death into the world by her disobedience, Mary helped to restore this original grace by giving birth to Christ, who offers us eternal life. Eve, the mother of all the living, is taken from the flesh of Adam. The New Adam (Christ) is taken from the flesh of Mary, the Mother of Life. Irenaeus believes that both Eve and Mary were virgins: this implies a state of physical and spiritual integrity as well as potential for growth. A parallel type, which Irenaeus also applies to Mary, is that of the untilled earth of paradise from which God fashioned Adam.[1]

The importance of this typology is that it reveals God's saving plan, or dispensation, from the beginning of creation. In creating

[1]Irenaeus of Lyons, *On the Apostolic Preaching* I.32, trans. J. Behr (Crestwood, NY: St Vladimir's Seminary Press, 1997), 61.

human beings 'according to' (κατά) his image and likeness, God bestowed on them the gift of free will (Gen 1.26). The role of the two virgins, Eve and Mary, in this plan is, according to Irenaeus, one of self-determination: they are linked because they each chose to act in response to God's commandment. Tragically, the former chose to disobey; however, her sin was overturned by Mary's decision to accept God's will. This happy outcome reveals not only humanity's ability to live up to its God-given potential, but also God's mercy in initiating the new dispensation. There is thus a double aspect to the Eve-Mary typology: it involves both the inherent goodness of both female figures, but also the free will that enabled them to make their choices. In this way, they represent the whole of humanity in its progress from grace to a fallen state, which was then redeemed in Jesus Christ.

The background for these ideas is Scripture, with the most explicit source being St Paul's emphasis on the fulfillment of the old dispensation in the new. He was also the first Christian writer to develop a typology of Christ as the "Second Adam," as we see in Romans 5.14–15:

> Yet death reigned from Adam to Moses, even over those whose sins were not like the transgression of Adam, who was a type of the one who was to come. But the free gift is not like the trespass. For if many died through one man's trespass, much more have the grace of God and the free gift in the grace of that one man Jesus Christ abounded for many.[2]

Although he thus saw Adam as a type for Christ, St Paul did not extend this imagery to Eve and Mary. For Irenaeus of Lyons, these

[2]See also 1 Corinthians 15.47: "The first man was of the earth, made of dust; the second man is the Lord from heaven."

female figures played a decisive role in the narrative of God's saving plan, according to the doctrine of "recapitulation," or the fulfillment of the old dispensation in the new. In this chapter, we will look first at this important second-century theologian's development of the theme and then explore its absorption into the Orthodox liturgical tradition. The typological understanding of Mary as the "Second Eve" is fundamental to the role that she played in Christ's Incarnation—and therefore in the salvation of all creation.

Irenaeus of Lyons and the doctrine of recapitulation

Irenaeus was an early Christian theologian whose work encapsulated the holistic nature of God's dispensation. Irenaeus stressed the goodness of creation, which God created out of nothing and which has the potential to be transfigured with divine grace. This potential was partially fulfilled by the Incarnation of Christ and reaches completion at his Second Coming. Irenaeus developed a uniquely Judaeo-Christian perspective of history, as opposed to the cyclical one that prevailed among pagans at the time that he was writing.[3] History, for Jews and Christians, began at the point when God created the universe out of nothing. It has developed according to a divine plan that leads towards fulfillment and salvation, although humanity has always played an essential role in this process, either disobeying its covenant with God or acting in accordance with his will. Irenaeus thus stresses both the inherent goodness of God's creation, but also the orderly way in which it will attain its full potential.

Irenaeus's concept of recapitulation is fundamental to his understanding of the divine dispensation. It provides the key for

[3]J. Pelikan, *Mary Through the Centuries. Her Place in the History of Culture* (New Haven, CT and London: Yale University Press, 1996), 39–41.

understanding why things that initially do not appear to make sense, such as Adam's and Eve's tasting of the fruit in paradise, actually form part of a larger narrative that is leading humanity towards salvation. The term "recapitulation" is in fact derived from a rhetorical background: it means "conclusion," that is, the final part of a text or speech in which ideas are summed up and conclusions are drawn. In theological terms, it designates what Irenaeus sees as the crucial event in Christian history, that is, the moment when God sent his Son, who emptied himself and became incarnate as Jesus of Nazareth. This was a historical moment, but it was also an event that God had known from the very beginning and towards which everything in the old dispensation was leading. Suddenly, when Christ assumed human nature, the meaning of those events could be understood. The creation of Adam, who was made of dust but had the potential to become divine, had been fulfilled in the person of Jesus Christ, the "Second Adam," who was fully human but also divine. Irenaeus explores this theological concept in detail, showing how the old dispensation is not only re-stated, or re-enacted, in the new, but is actually fulfilled in all its original promise. Just as Adam in some sense represented humanity, and thereby conferred on us his fallen condition, so did Christ restore to all of us that original blessed state—as well as the potential to become what God originally intended us to be. This recapitulation of human nature in Christ thus represents both the closing of a chapter of human history and the opening of the next installment, in which those who follow Christ are granted life in his body by the grace of the Holy Spirit.

Some scholars have emphasized the extent to which Irenaeus of Lyons was affected by heresies that were propounding alternative ideas about Christ and salvation towards the end of the second century.[4] Such heresies included the diverse teachings of groups that are commonly designated "gnostic," as well as those known as "adoptionist." Whereas some gnostic teachers propounded docetist ideas, according to which Christ, as God and Savior, only appeared to take on the body of a human being, the adoptionists denied his eternal nature as Son and Word of God.[5] It is certainly true that Irenaeus had polemical reasons for attempting a systematic explanation of Orthodox Christian theology; his five-volume work, entitled *Against the Heresies,* is a testament to his commitment to combat such subversive views.[6] However, his shorter treatise, *On the Apostolic Preaching,* was intended as a summary of Christian doctrine for a faithful audience. There can be no doubt that Irenaeus developed his doctrine of recapitulation, which is based above all on Biblical revelation, in order to help Christians both to understand the narrative that informed their rule of faith and to model their lives on its teaching. The

[4]See, for example, R.M. Grant, *Irenaeus* (London and New York: Routledge, 1997), 1–45; D. Minns, *Irenaeus. An Introduction* (London and New York: T. & T. Clark International, 2010), 15–29.

[5]At first glance, these two positions seem similar; however, they differ slightly in their emphasis. Many Gnostics taught that Jesus Christ was an apparition; thus his disciples thought that he was truly present but were in fact only seeing a vision of their Savior. The adoptionists meanwhile believed that Christ's spirit entered the body of the man Jesus, but was never fully subsumed into that nature. For background, see J. Behr, *Formation of Christian Theology,* vol. 1: *The Way to Nicaea* (Crestwood, NY: St Vladimir's Seminary Press, 2001), 76–77, 83–84, 142–43.

[6]Irenaeus of Lyons' *Against Heresies* is available in translation in A.C. Coxe, J. Donaldson, and A. Roberts, eds., Ante-Nicene Fathers: The Writings of the Fathers down to AD 325 (Edinburgh: T. & T. Clark; repr. Grand Rapids: Eerdmans, 1985–87) [hereafter ANF], vol. 1, 315–578.

confidence with which Irenaeus employed the typology and concept of recapitulation suggests that it was not a recent invention. Nevertheless, whereas St Paul and Justin Martyr had juxtaposed the old and new dispensations, highlighting types and antitypes such as Adam and Christ, in a similar way, they did not work it out in detail to the extent that Irenaeus did, especially in his treatise, *On the Apostolic Preaching*.

It is worth examining Irenaeus's understanding of the typological connection between Eve and Mary in detail because it has significant implications from a Mariological point of view. Let us explore first how Irenaeus describes Mary's role in recapitulating Eve's transgression. Having arrived at the turning point in his narrative of Old and New Testament history, when God became incarnate of a virgin, he describes this event in the following words:

> And just as through a disobedient virgin man was struck and, falling, died, so also by means of a virgin, who obeyed the word of God, man, being revivified, received life. For the Lord came to seek back the lost sheep, and it was man who was lost; and therefore, he did not become any other formation, but [being born] from her who was of the race of Adam, he maintained the likeness of the formation. For it was necessary for Adam to be recapitulated in Christ, that "mortality might be swallowed up in immortality" (cf. 2 Cor 5.4; 1 Cor 15.54); and Eve in Mary, that a virgin, become an advocate for a virgin, might undo and destroy the virginal disobedience by virginal obedience.[7]

What immediately strikes us in this passage is Irenaeus's focus on the two virgins, Eve and Mary, as significant actors in this story.

[7]Irenaeus, *On the Apostolic Preaching* I.33, trans. Behr, 61.

It is "through a disobedient virgin" (Eve) that man fell, but her sin is undone or "loosed from its knot," as Irenaeus describes it elsewhere,[8] by the Virgin Mary. The description of Mary as "advocate" in this passage is worthy of comment. Irenaeus probably used the Greek παράκλητος here, which can mean "advocate" or "intercessor," as in a court of law.[9] Later the word became associated with the Holy Spirit and is often translated "comforter" or "consoler." In this context, where Irenaeus is describing how Mary's obedience to God's will overturned Eve's error, it is the intercessory sense that prevails. Most importantly, however, Irenaeus draws our attention to the freedom with which each woman acted out her role in the narrative. Thus, as we saw earlier, the recapitulation that took place in Christ's Incarnation was based on two factors: God's all-merciful act of condescension and the willingness on the part of humanity (represented by the Virgin Mary) to participate in this mystery.

One other aspect of Irenaeus's portrayal of Eve is significant with regard to the doctrine of recapitulation. This is her role as Adam's partner and helper, without whom he would not attain his full potential as a human being. Matthew Steenberg suggests that Irenaeus balances the typological correspondence of Adam and Christ with that of Eve and Mary for theological, not purely aesthetic, reasons.[10] God created Eve as Adam's "helper" who was

[8]Irenaeus, *Against the Heresies* III.22.4, ANF, vol. 1, 455.

[9]Irenaeus uses the same term in *Against the Heresies* V.19.1, ANF, vol. 1, 547. See the discussion of these passages in L. Gambero, *Mary and the Fathers of the Church. The Blessed Virgin Mary in Patristic Thought* (San Francisco, CA: Ignatius Press, 1999), 56.

[10]M.C. Steenberg, "The Role of Mary as Co-recapitulator in St Irenaeus of Lyons," *Vigiliae Christianae* 58, no. 2 (May 2004), 117–37.

"comparable with him" and with whom he would "become one flesh" (Gen 2.20, 24). The Biblical text suggests that this was a partnership on equal terms—to the extent that any partnership is truly egalitarian, that is—with the implication that God intended Adam and Eve to grow together into the spiritual maturity that awaited them. Eve would play an active role in this process as Adam's "helper"; unfortunately, she instead used that initiative to lead him astray when she chose to follow the advice of the serpent. Eve's and Mary's roles in the recapitulative theory of God's dispensation have to do with their exercising of free will, as opposed to the more ontological correspondence between Adam and Christ. Thus, for Irenaeus, the Adam-Christ typology represents God's creative act, first in forming humanity and then in recapitulating it, while the Eve-Mary parallel represents the human dimension in this dispensation. Salvation will occur not merely by divine command; humanity must play its part by responding and accepting that gift of eternal life.

Eve-Mary Typology in Patristic and Byzantine tradition

The typological link between Eve and Mary continued to be emphasized in the Patristic period, eventually making its way into the liturgical tradition that developed especially in connection with the great Marian feasts. One of the most productive and imaginative of the fourth-century theologians, who flourished in the Eastern territories of the Roman empire, was the Syriac poet, St Ephrem. Typology and poetic imagery are embraced by this writer: in his many surviving hymns and verse homilies, known as *madrashe* and *memre*, respectively, the poet "clothes" divine revelation in images that are drawn from well-known Old Testament types, prophecy, and daily life. As Sebastian Brock remarks, St Ephrem is a theologian with a holistic vision of creation: God makes himself known to humanity not only by means of words, especially as revealed in Scripture, but also through his creation.[11] Those who are faithful, and who have worked to purify their hearts so as to gain a clear vision of this truth, may discern these signs (*raze*) of God's immanence.

St Ephrem's cycle of hymns, *On the Nativity*, frequently emphasizes Mary's central role in the Incarnation of Christ. In one of these, putting words into the Virgin's mouth as she addresses Christ, the poet writes:

> In her virginity, Eve put on
> Leaves of shame, but your mother has put on,
> In her virginity, a robe of glory
> That encompasses all, while to him who covers all
> She gives a body as a tiny garment.[12]

And in one of a series of hymns titled, *On the Church*, he states:

> Mary and Eve in their symbols
> Resemble a body, one of whose eyes
> Is blind and darkened.
> While the other is bright and clear,
> Providing light for the whole.[13]

---

[11]See, for example, S. Brock, trans., *St Ephrem the Syrian, Hymns on Paradise* (Crestwood, NY: St Vladimir's Seminary Press, 1990), 39–49; idem, *Moran 'Etho. Bride of Light* (Kottayam, India: St Ephrem Ecumenical Research Institute, 1994), 1–9.

[12]Ephrem, *Hymns on the Nativity* 17, trans. Brock, *Bride of Light*, 25.

[13]Ephrem, *Hymns on the Church* 37, ibid., 31.

Early Byzantine writers, such as the fifth-century Proclus of Constantinople, also employed typology in a poetic way, as they explored the meaning of Eve's and Mary's contrasting roles in the divine dispensation. Proclus writes, for example, in a homily on the holy Theotokos that was delivered in the Great Church in Constantinople at the very time that the patriarch Nestorius was questioning her importance in the Incarnation of Christ, as follows:

> Through ears that disobeyed, the serpent poured in his
>   poison;
> Through ears that obeyed, the Word entered in order to
>   build a living temple.[14]

Both Ephrem and Proclus stress the antithetical connection between Eve and Mary by means of parallel, rhythmic phrases: whereas Eve was deceived by the serpent and turned away from God, Mary listened to the archangel's message and accepted salvation. Nicholas Constas has explored Proclus's imaginative use of the widespread belief that the Virgin Mary conceived Christ through her ear, or sense of hearing (δι᾽ ἀκοῆς). In another homily, Proclus writes, "An angel appeared and arrayed me without corruption in the garments of a bride, and I heard a word, I conceived a Word, and I delivered a Word."[15] The theological elegance of this formulation scarcely needs emphasizing. God has made himself known throughout history by means of his Word; he remains the Word in his Incarnation. How fitting, therefore that he should

---

[14]Proclus of Constantinople, *Homily* I.ii, trans. N. Constas, *Proclus of Constantinople and the Cult of the Virgin in Late Antiquity. Homilies 1–5, Texts and Translations* (Leiden, Boston, and Cologne: Brill, 2003), 139.

[15]Constas, *Proclus of Constantinople*, 280.

be conceived by means of a word that was uttered, by the agency of an angel, into the ear of the Virgin Mary! This understanding of Christ's conception continues to appear in the writings of later Byzantine liturgical writers, including Romanos the Melodist, John of Damascus, and Andrew of Crete. Nor is the typological parallel between Eve and Mary ever forgotten in this image. The conception of Christ is linked with Mary's willing acceptance of God's word; this can be contrasted with Eve's fatal acceptance of the deceiver's word.

One further elaboration of this parallel is the contrast made by some Patristic writers between Mary, as pure bride of Christ, with Eve who, in metaphorical terms, committed adultery with the serpent. A Syriac writer, Narsai of Edessa writes, for example:

> At the beginning of time, the envious one was unable to deceive man, so he chose a serpent to contain his bitterness, and strummed, as if to the strains of a lyre, on the strings of the flesh. He entranced the serpent, and composed a rhapsody for the woman, who found it soothing, and accepted its counsel. On a flute of flesh, the deceiver chanted the words of deception. Through a material voice, he cultivated the ears of the weak woman, and the slanderer deposited his seed deep within her soul.[16]

The Theotokos of course overturned, or compensated for, Eve's sinful promiscuity, as she did her disobedience. Later Byzantine writers, such as the tenth-century John Geometres, developed bridal imagery in connection with Mary's role in the Incarnation to an even greater extent, describing the Annunciation as the moment at which the Word and humanity entered into a "mystical

[16]Quoted and translated in Constas, *Proclus of Constantinople*, 284.

and ineffable alliance."[17] It is also worth emphasizing here that the Virgin's free acceptance of this marriage with Christ is an essential feature in the narrative. In a fourteenth-century sermon on the Annunciation, Nicholas Cabasilas shows how the story of the Annunciation recapitulates God's creation of the world and of the first man, Adam. He emphasizes that it was the Virgin Mary's, words, "Let it be unto me according to your word" (Lk 1.38), that allowed the Word to become flesh and to dwell among us (cf. Jn 1.14).[18]

Byzantine Hymnography: The *Akathistos Hymn*

Some Patristic texts have experienced a long life in Orthodox Christian tradition, since they were incorporated into the liturgical services that continue to be celebrated today. One of the earliest texts to enjoy this status is the fifth- or sixth-century *Akathistos Hymn*, which may be sung on the first four Fridays in Lent, but especially in Matins on the so-called "Akathistos Saturday" at the end of the fifth week.[19] The author and precise origins of the hymn remain unknown, although scholars have suggested dates between the early fifth and seventh centuries, with some believing that it

[17]John Geometres, *On the Annunciation*, PG 106, col. 820.

[18]Nicholas Cabasilas, *On the Annunciation*, ed. M. Jugie, *Homélies mariales byzantines*, PO 19, fasc. 3, no. 93 (Paris: R. Graffin, 1925; repr. Turnhout: Brepols, 1990), 487–88. I am indebted for this reference once again to Constas, *Proclus of Constantinople*, 306, who provides an excellent discussion of its theological implications.

[19]In some churches, the hymn is also divided into four parts and sung on the first four Fridays of Lent. See Mother Mary and Archimandrite Kallistos Ware, trans., *The Lenten Triodion* (London: Faber and Faber, 1969; repr. S. Canaan, PA: St Tikhon's Seminary Press, 2002), 55.

should be attributed to the famous sixth-century hymnographer, Romanos the Melodist.[20] The *Akathistos* is remarkable both for its Christological focus on the Theotokos and for its rich use of typology and imagery in connection with this exalted subject. The theme of Mary as "Second Eve" features prominently, as the hymnographer relates the fulfillment of the old dispensation in the new. The first stanza, for example, after opening with a short narrative about the Annunciation, reminds us of the change that Mary brings about in her acceptance of God's will, as the angel cries:

> Hail, for through you joy shall shine forth;
> Hail, for through you the curse shall cease;
> Hail, recalling of fallen Adam;
> Hail, deliverance from the tears of Eve . . .[21]

The juxtaposition of bridal imagery with the Virgin's decision is ubiquitous in this text too. Each stanza ends with the refrain, "Hail, bride unwedded," which reminds us both of Mary's virginal state but also of her union with the Bridegroom, Christ. The transition from sin to deliverance, darkness to light, the law to grace, and related themes is celebrated throughout the hymn. The Virgin Mary is portrayed as the catalyst, or vehicle, through which this change takes place. She is the one who brings "opposites to harmony," through whom "our sin is remitted," and through whom "Paradise is opened."[22]

[20]For example, P. Maas, "Die Chronologie der Hymnen des Romanos," *Byzantinische Zeitschrift* 15 (1906), 1, ff.; E. Wellesz, "The 'Akathistos'. A Study in Byzantine Hymnography," *Dumbarton Oaks Papers* 9/10 (1956), esp. 152–53.

[21]*The Akathistos Hymn, Ikos One*, trans. Mother Mary and Archimandrite Kallistos Ware, *Lenten Triodion*, 423 (with adjustments).

[22]*The Akathistos Hymn, Ikos Eight*, ibid., 429.

One further symbolic association that is connected with Mary's role as "Second Eve" is the notion that her womb represents the baptismal font. The womb of the Theotokos contained the God who is uncontainable; it is also the place where human redemption began. When catechumens are baptized into the Church, they participate in the union of divinity and humanity that occurred in Mary's womb, becoming one with the body of Christ. The *Akathistos Hymn* explores this symbolism in passages such as the following one:

> Hail, for you prefigure the baptismal font:
> Hail, for you take away the filth of sin.
> Hail, water washing clean the conscience:
> Hail, cup wherein is mixed the wine of mighty joy.[23]

Leena Mari Peltomaa, in a recent study of the *Akathistos Hymn*, has pointed out parallels in the use of such imagery with Patristic writers such as Didymus of Alexandria and Proclus of Constantinople. The former, in a passage that explicitly connects Mary's role as baptismal font with her undoing of Eve's sin, writes as follows:

> For [Mary] is the baptismal font of the Trinity, the workshop of salvation of all believers; and those who bathe therein she frees from the bite of the serpent and she becomes mother of all, a virgin dwelling in the Holy Spirit . . .[24]

---

[23]*The Akathistos Hymn, Ikos Eleven*, ibid., 435 (with adjustments).

[24]Didymus of Alexandria, *On the Trinity* II.xiii, PG 39, col. 692; trans. L.M. Peltomaa, *The Image of the Virgin Mary in the Akathistos Hymn* (Leiden, Boston, and Cologne: Brill, 2001), 132–3.

Byzantine hymnography:
The Feast of the Annunciation

The hymns that adorn the liturgical feasts of the Mother of God were mostly composed from about the eighth century onward. They are based on Scriptural exegesis that had been developing, as we have seen, from the first centuries of the Church. Middle Byzantine preachers and hymnographers condensed and organized such reflection into readings and hymns for the Marian feasts soon after their institution in the calendar for the fixed liturgical year. As we saw in Chapter One and will continue to explore in the course of this book, typology features prominently in Orthodox liturgical praise of the Mother of God. Certain types, such as Jacob's ladder, the Burning Bush, Gideon's Fleece, and the Tabernacle or Temple (along with much of their furniture) feature prominently; it is interesting, too, that some are associated more with particular feasts than others.[25]

Typology involving Eve and Mary is employed most frequently in the liturgical texts for the feast of the Annunciation (March 25). This feast celebrates the event when the parallel between the two figures is most obvious: Mary accepted the word of God whereas Eve disobeyed it. There is a strong narrative element in this feast too: the hymns that are sung in the vigil services tell the story, based on the first chapter of Luke's Gospel, of the archangel Gabriel's descent to Nazareth and his greeting to the Virgin Mary. Basing themselves on a long-standing tradition of dialogue hymns

---

[25]For example, types involving the temple are particularly appropriate for the feast of Mary's Entry in the Temple, for obvious reasons. For an excellent study of Marian typology and its placement in the feasts, see P. Ladouceur, "Old Testament Prefigurations of the Mother of God," *St Vladimir's Theological Quarterly* 50, nos. 1–2 (2006), 5–57.

and homilies that were written in honor of this event, the eighth-century hymnographers express this narrative by means of an imagined dialogue between Gabriel and Mary. Thus, in Gabriel's first speech to the Virgin, according to Kosmas the Melodist, he might have spoken as follows:

> Hail, O unwedded maiden who have not known marriage. Do not be struck with dismay by my strange form, nor be afraid: I am an archangel. Once the serpent beguiled Eve, but now I announce to you the good tidings of joy: O most pure, you will remain inviolate and yet will bear the Lord.[26]

Luke's Gospel does of course recount the conversation that took place between the archangel and Mary. Later liturgical writers elaborated on this, inventing further speeches both for theological and dramatic reasons. The Virgin's doubt, for example, on encountering this strange apparition, reflects her desire not to be led astray as her ancestor Eve was; there is a real risk that, as in the previous case, this may be the devil in disguise who has come to tempt her into disobedience and sin. Gradually, according to the narratives of Byzantine liturgical writers, the archangel Gabriel manages to persuade her of his divine origin and to prepare her for her mysterious role as Birth-Giver of God. What hymnographers and preachers are above all attempting to do, as they extend this dialogue, is to show Christians how Mary wrestled with this momentous decision and grew in spiritual maturity in the course of her conversation with Gabriel. The dramatic portrayal of the scene helps the faithful to identify with the Virgin and to understand her true humanity. Parts of John of Damascus's kanon for the office of

---

[26]Mother Mary and Archimandrite Kallistos Ware, trans., *The Festal Menaion*, 444 (with adjustments).

Matins are written in dialogue form and may be sung antiphonally by separate choirs or individual singers. After Gabriel arrives and greets her, in the course of the first Ode, Mary replies:

> O Angel, help me to understand the meaning of your words. How shall what you say come to pass? Tell me clearly, how shall I conceive, who am a virgin maid? And how shall I become the Mother of my Maker?

Later in the same hymn, after further speeches between the two figures, the Virgin expresses her fear of falling into the same trap that Eve did:

> My mother Eve, accepting the suggestion of the serpent, was banished from divine delight: and therefore I fear your strange salutation, for I take heed lest I slip.[27]

As liturgical writers such as John proceed to make clear in the course of the offices and liturgy for the feast of the Annunciation, Mary's final decision had momentous consequences. Not only did she avoid Eve's mistake, by making sure of the archangel's credentials and authentic message, but she also reversed that transgression by accepting her role as Theotokos. That this decision was based on rational consent, as well as on the prophesied destiny of this holy Virgin, is underlined in every liturgical text that is associated with the feast.

The joyous consequences of Mary's decision, which represent the beginning of redemption for all creation, are celebrated in hymns

---

[27]Mother Mary and Archimandrite Kallistos Ware, *The Festal Menaion*, 449–50 (with adjustments). The translators note that some editions of the service books ascribe only Canticles Eight and Nine to John, and the remainder of the Kanon to Theophanes.

such as the following sticheron (verse), written by the ninth-century hymnographer, Theophanes Graptos:

> Today is revealed the mystery that is from all eternity. The Son of God becomes the Son of man, that, sharing in what is worse, he may make me share in what is better. In times of old Adam was once deceived: he sought to become God, but received not his desire. Now God becomes man, that he may make Adam God. Let creation rejoice, let nature exult: for the Archangel stands in fear before the Virgin and, saying to her "Hail," he brings the joyful greeting whereby our sorrow is assuaged . . . [28]

Conclusion: Mary, "the Mother of Life"

The Greek Septuagint translates the Hebrew name "Eve" literally as "Life" (ζωή) in Genesis 3.20: "And Adam called the name of his wife 'Life', because she was the Mother of all the Living." Clement of Alexandria, writing in the second century, commented on this passage as follows:

> The woman who initiated transgression was called "Life," because she was responsible for the succession of those who came to birth and sinned. She thus became mother of the righteous and unrighteous alike. Each one of us shows himself to be just or willfully renders himself disobedient.[29]

---

[28]Mother Mary and Archimandrite Kallistos Ware, *The Festal Menaion*, 460.

[29]Clement of Alexandria, *Stromateis* III.65.1; translated in A. Louth, ed., *Ancient Christian Commentary on Scripture. Old Testament, vol. 1: Genesis 1–11* (Chicago and London: Fitzroy Dearborn Publishers, 2001), 98.

In other words, and as both Scripture and the Fathers tell us, Eve became the biological mother of the human race. Whether or not we believe this in literal terms, we may understand its implications with regard to a common inheritance. This inheritance includes a noble origin, since God made us according to his image and likeness (Gen 1.26) and thereby gave us free will. However, each of us possesses the ability to commit good or evil acts. The tragic story of human history, as recounted in the Old Testament, testifies repeatedly to Israel's failure to live up to its original promise or to its covenant with God.

Mary, the Mother of God, as "Second Eve," recapitulated Eve's nature and fateful decision. In other words, she was human, and she was a virgin, as was Eve before the fall, but instead of choosing to disobey God, Mary chose to do his will. She accepted his word and conceived Christ, the divine Word, who became incarnate in her womb. The consequences of this action, which result from both from the grace with which this Virgin was endowed and from her own free will, are as significant for the rest of humanity—and indeed all creation—as those of Eve. The Incarnation brought redemption from death and the inherited sin, along with the hope of future salvation. It is for this reason that Mary is hailed in many liturgical texts as "the Mother of Joy" or even as "the Mother of Life."[30] The latter epithet alludes typologically to Eve, who was the "Mother of all the Living." However, it refers at the same time to the fact that Mary gave birth to the Life of the world, Christ himself. She thus helped to bring about, through him, eternal life for all those who accept his Word.

[30]Mother Mary and Archimandrite Kallistos Ware, *The Festal Menaion*, 441 (with adjustments): "Hail, O pure Virgin; hail, Bride unwedded. Hail, Mother of Life: blessed is the fruit of your womb."

Further Reading:

Irenaeus of Lyons. *On the Apostolic Preaching* I.32, trans. John Behr. Crestwood, NY: St Vladimir's Seminary Press, 1997.

Minns, Denis. *Irenaeus. An Introduction.* London and New York: T. & T. Clark International, 2010.

Pelikan, Jaroslav. *Mary Through the Centuries. Her Place in the History of Culture.* New Haven, CT and London: Yale University Press, 1996, Chapter 3: "The Second Eve and the Guarantee of Christ's True Humanity."

Steenberg, Matthew C. *Of God and Man. Theology as Anthropology from Irenaeus to Athanasius.* London and New York: Continuum, 2009.

Steenberg, Matthew C. "The Role of Mary as Co-Recapitulator in St Irenaeus of Lyons," *Vigiliae Christianae* 58, no. 2 (May 2004), 117–37.

chapter four

VIRGINITY AND THE MOTHER OF GOD

One of the aspects of the Mother of God that is central to Orthodox Christian tradition is her virginity. Liturgical texts stress this doctrine both explicitly and by means of types or poetic images. A hymn that is sung in the midnight office on Saturday evening expresses the theological importance of Mary's virginity in the following way:

> You conceived without seed, and ineffably you bore the One who put down the mighty from their throne and exalts the humble and raises the horn of his faithful ones, who glorify the Cross and the Tomb and the glorious Resurrection of Christ . . .[1]

This passage conveys the mystery that is associated with this state; it is seen as a sign of the divinity that was contained in Mary's womb. The prophets, especially Isaiah, foretold Mary's virginity;[2] Patristic writers also understood this as a sign of the

[1] Trans. Archimandrite Ephrem Lash, Dogmatikon in Tone 4, Saturday Small Vespers, at <http://www.anastasis.org.uk/sat4ec.htm>.

[2] As we saw in Chapter One, pp. 25–26, there is ambiguity with regard to Mary's virginity in the text of Isaiah 7.14 in the Hebrew Bible. However, the

mystery of divine being. Typology is also used in liturgical texts to express Mary's pure and uncorrupted condition. Old Testament signs such as the burning bush (Ex 3.1–8) and the closed gate of Solomon's temple (Ezek 43.27–44.4), as we shall see later in this chapter, indicate that the Son of God entered Mary's womb while leaving her virginity intact.

Orthodox Christian tradition calls the Virgin Mary "Theotokos" ("Birth-giver of God") without distinguishing between the various phases of her youth, birth-giving, and subsequent life. Mary is understood to be virginal—in every sense of the word—throughout this period; such purity is essential to her miraculous role and indeed to the mystery of the Incarnation itself. However, it is worth highlighting here, for the sake of clarity, some distinctions with regard to this blessed state that have emerged in the course of Christian history—especially in the Western Churches. Some commentators point to three separate phases in Mary's virginity: first, that which exists before her conception of the Word of God (as recounted in the Gospels of Matthew and Luke); second, the intact physical state (known as "virginity *in partu*") that obtained after Mary's delivery of the Christ child; and third, her continuing chastity in later life (known as "virginity *post partum*"). Whereas some Christian Churches, especially Protestant ones, may accept Mary's virginal conception of Christ, they may not believe in her virginity *in partu* or *post partum* because these are not clearly attested in the canonical New Testament.

Greek Septuagint, which has served as inspired Scripture in the Christian Church from its beginnings, clearly describes the Mother of God as 'virgin' (παρθένος). This is picked up in the Gospels of Luke and Matthew, followed by other early Christian writers.

The Orthodox and Roman Catholic Churches see all three phases as bound up in the doctrine of Christ's Incarnation as God-man. Mary as Theotokos or Mother of God was known to God from the beginning, as the Old Testament attests. She was—and remains—the holy receptacle that fulfilled the promise of the Incarnation. It is also worth emphasizing that the title "Theotokos" refers, both in Patristic and modern Orthodox Christian thought, to the whole process of conception and child-bearing: it is thus impossible, according to this tradition, to distinguish separate phases in this process. Virginity is an essential element in the narrative, as we shall see in this chapter. It refers both to Mary's spiritual and physical state, as the one who accepts her role as Birth-giver of God, and to the ontological mystery itself. The first aspect is, as it were, a prerequisite of the second, so we shall treat them in that order—even as we remember that they are each a part of the same question.

Some Historical Background

If we begin with the earliest Christian traditions concerning Christ's birth from a young woman named Mary, we see that the Evangelists Matthew and Luke, followed by post-Apostolic and Patristic writers, unanimously affirmed her virginity at the time that she conceived Christ. In the Gospel of Luke, Mary exclaims to the archangel Gabriel, "How can this be, since I do not know a man?" (Lk 1.34). About a generation later, St Ignatius of Antioch wrote as follows concerning this miraculous conception:

> Mary's virginity was hidden from the prince of this world;[3]
> so was her child-bearing, and so was the death of the Lord.

[3] Cf. I Corinthians 1.20.

All these three trumpet-tongued secrets were brought to pass in the deep silence of the Lord.[4]

Justin Martyr, writing before AD 165, defended the reality of the virgin birth—meaning Mary's virginal state at the time of the conception of Christ—in his *Dialogue with Trypho*. He argued not only that the Septuagint version of Isaiah's prophecy is legitimate, but also that such a miracle is fitting for the birth of the Son of God.[5]

It is noticeable, in spite of the unity of later Orthodox tradition concerning Mary's perpetual virginity (as noted above), that some early Christian writers expressed diverse views concerning the nature of her birth-giving and about her subsequent life. It is possible that such variation reflected a desire to oppose particular heresies, either by stressing the normality of Christ's birth or by upholding its supernatural quality.[6] It was ultimately the latter position that gained acceptance as official doctrine, especially after the decisions of the first ecumenical Council at Nicaea in AD 325.

Many early texts do, however, affirm the mystery of Mary's continuing virginity throughout the conception, gestation, and

[4]Ignatius of Antioch, *Letter to the Ephesians* 19, trans. M. Staniforth, *Early Christian Writings: The Apostolic Fathers* (London: Penguin Books, 1987), 66.

[5]Justin Martyr, *Dialogue with Trypho* 43 and 67, trans. T.B. Falls, *Writings of St Justin Martyr* (Washington, DC: Catholic University of America Press, 1948; repr. 1977), 212–13; 254–6.

[6]See, for example, Tertullian's detailed discussion of the natural process of Christ's gestation and birth in his treatise, *On the Flesh of Christ* 23, trans. G. Dunne, "Mary's Virginity *in partu* and Tertullian's Anti-Docetism in *De carne Christi* Reconsidered," *Journal of Theological Studies*, n.s. 58, Part 2 (2007), 480. Such a position may have been adopted in opposition to gnostic or docetist teachings that denied Christ's physical incarnation.

birth of Christ. The second-century *Protevangelium of James*, for example, is one of the strongest witnesses to this tradition. The text underlines Mary's intact physical state by telling the story of Salome, the midwife, who insisted on inspecting her after the birth. By using such a witness, the author intends to eliminate any doubts in the minds of his readers concerning the miraculous nature of this birth. However, he also uses this passage to make a more subtle theological point. Physical proof should not be necessary when God manifests himself to humanity in creation. Salome is punished for 'tempting God' to provide such proof; on repenting and declaring her faith in Christ, the King and Messiah, her hand is restored.[7]

A century or two later, most Christian writers had come to accept the extraordinary—or virginal—nature of Christ's mysterious conception and birth from the Virgin Mary. This was an event that, while revealing his physical nature and true humanity, involved the entrance of the Son of God into creation. The Cappadocian Fathers were united in their support of the doctrine of Mary's virginity *in partu*. They believed that God's begetting of Christ, in a pure and virginal manner from Mary, mirrored his eternal generation as the Word.[8] This was also a gestation and birth that

[7]There may be an allusion here to the story of the doubting Thomas (Jn 20. 24–29), although the Evangelist John does not suggest any punishment for the Apostle in this instance. An even closer parallel may be found in the story of Jephonias, the doubting Jew who touched the bier of the Mother of God as it was being carried towards the tomb in Gethsemane and lost his hand, according to certain accounts of her "falling asleep" and burial. See above, pp. 59–60. Like Salome, the midwife, Jephonias's hand was restored after he declared his faith in Christ.

[8]For an excellent examination of this subject, see V.E.F. Harrison, "Gender, Generation, and Virginity in Cappadocian Theology," *Journal of Theological Studies*, n.s. 47, Part 1 (1996), 38–68.

involved no physical pain, as we see in the following statement by Gregory of Nyssa:

> [Christ's] conception did not result from the union of two humans; his birth was not polluted in any way; there were no labor pangs . . . In fact, his birth alone occurred without labor pains, and he alone began to exist without sexual relations. Indeed, for her who remained incorrupt and who had no knowledge of such relations, the word "birth" does not seem appropriate, because virginity and birth do not go together.[9]

This reversal of nature, as far as Mary is concerned, was also seen as reversing Eve's punishment of bringing forth children "in pain," according to Genesis 3.16.

Belief in the essential fact of Mary's virginity in association with Christ's birth was universally accepted in both Eastern and Western Christendom by the end of the fourth century. The issue would be explored further in connection with Christological controversies in the course of the next century, with the Theotokos playing a central role in these discussions. Before discussing Mary's virginity in this doctrinal context, however, it is worth saying something about what we might call the "moral" aspect of the question. To what extent is virginity a necessary spiritual, or personal, quality for the Mother of God? And what is the specific position of Orthodox Christian tradition on this question?

---

[9]Gregory of Nyssa, *On the Song of Songs* 13, trans. L. Gambero, *Mary and the Fathers of the Church. The Blessed Virgin Mary in Patristic Thought* (San Francisco, CA: Ignatius Press, 1999), 158.

The Moral Aspect of Mary's Virginity

"Blessed are the pure in heart, for they shall see God" (Mt 5.8). This teaching, which Jesus expressed to the crowd on a mountain in Galilee, sums up the Orthodox view of the Mother of God. She is continually described in liturgical texts as "all-pure," "holy," and, as the archangel Gabriel—as well as the hymns that are based on his salutation—put it, "full of grace." Narratives such as the *Protevangelium of James* provide theological background for such statements. According to this text, Mary was guarded carefully in her mother Anna's bedchamber until the age of three; after this she was raised in the holy precincts of the Jewish temple where she was fed by the hand of an angel. Going back even beyond this period in Mary's life, her purity and fitness to become Mother of Christ was foretold in the Old Testament by the prophets and by mysterious types, as we have seen. Mary, because of her purity in heart, was receptive to God's word when she encountered the archangel Gabriel. She was not hindered by the selfish preoccupations and tendency to sin that afflict the rest of humanity. The Theotokos represents, in Orthodox Christian tradition, a paradigm of the innocent human nature that God created in the beginning. She is able to act independently, using her free will, but her actions are in tune with the purpose of her Creator as he seeks to restore humanity to its potential glory.

Patristic and liturgical texts associate Mary's physical virginity metaphorically with moral purity. John of Damascus, in a sermon on the Virgin's Nativity, writes, for example:

> [She is] a precious vessel of virginity who was a virgin before giving birth, a virgin during the birth-giving, and a virgin

after having given birth; she alone is virgin and ever-virgin; she alone forever remains a virgin in mind and soul and body . . . [10]

And later in the same homily, he continues:

> Hail, Mary, sweetest little daughter of Anna! . . . How shall I describe your most pious bearing, your robe, your gracious countenance! [You possessed] mature judgment in a youthful body. Your modest dress escaped all softness and delicacy. Your gait was pious and undisturbed, free from foolish ostentation. Your manner was austere, but mixed with gaiety; you were unapproachable by men—a witness to this is the fear that came over you at the unaccustomed address of the angel. [You were] docile and obedient towards your parents, while your humble mind was engaged in the highest contemplation. Your cheerful speech came forth from a soul that was free of anger . . .[11]

It is worth remembering, with respect to the Fathers' emphasis on the virtue that is associated with Mary's virginal state, that asceticism, and the celibacy that it entails, was highly prized in the early Church. The fourth century saw the development of the ascetic movement, beginning in Egypt, in which many Christians chose to leave the world and to devote their lives to ascetic training and prayer. It is thus no accident that it was precisely in this period that Christian writers began to portray Mary as the perfect model for those engaged in the monastic way of life, and especially for

[10]John of Damascus, *On the Nativity of the Holy Theotokos* 5, trans. M.B. Cunningham, *Wider Than Heaven. Eighth-Century Homilies on the Mother of God* (Crestwood, NY: St Vladimir's Seminary Press, 2008), 59.

[11]Ibid. 11, 69.

female virgins who had begun living together in communities—or occasionally even on their own.

Athanasius of Alexandria, in a letter addressed to a community of nuns, provides a long description of the young Virgin Mary, whom he imagines leading a pious life in her parents' house:

> Thus, Mary was a holy virgin, having the disposition of her soul balanced and doubly increasing. For she desired good works, doing what is proper, having true thoughts in faith and purity. And she did not desire to be seen by people; rather, she prayed that God would be her judge. Nor did she have an eagerness to leave her house, nor was she at all acquainted with the streets; rather, she remained in her house being calm, imitating the fly in honey. She virtuously spent the excess of her manual labor on the poor. And she did not acquire eagerness to look out the window, rather to look at the Scriptures. And she would pray to God privately, taking care about these two things: that she not let evil thoughts dwell in her heart, and also that she not acquire curiosity or learn hardness of heart . . . Straining forward daily, she made progress (cf. Philem 3.13). When she first arose, she strove that her works might be new, beyond what she had already done. She forgot her good works and her merciful deeds: she did them secretly. But she remembered the Lord, struggling to add to what she had done before, and the works of this age she removed from her heart. And she was not anxious about death; rather, she grieved and sighed daily that she had not yet entered the gates of heaven.[12]

[12]Athanasius of Alexandria, *First Letter to Virgins* 12–13, trans. D. Brakke, *Athanasius and Asceticism* (Baltimore and London: Johns Hopkins University Press, 1995), 277–8.

Athanasius portrays the Virgin Mary here as a normal young woman who is advancing in her spiritual life. She struggles to conquer evil thoughts and to impose discipline on herself in the same way that any other young virgin might have done. This image of the Theotokos is highly positive: Athanasius presents her as a model for other young virgins to follow. She is, in other words, the first ascetic saint in the Christian Church, choosing to devote her life to God as a "bride of Christ."

More recently, Orthodox theologians have described Mary, the Mother of God, as one who "expresses most perfectly [the] royal and universal priesthood" (1 Pet 2.9) that is the prerogative of all Christians. Metropolitan Kallistos Ware cites G.K. Chesterton's memorable aphorism, "Men are men, but Man is a woman," in connection with the blessed Virgin Mary.[13] She leads the way for all Christians in praising and glorifying God for the gift of creation and thereby turning her encounters with him into sacramental acts of thanksgiving. She presents her own body, which is sanctified by his grace and by her own pure way of life, as a living temple for the uncreated Word of God. This role, which the Theotokos fulfilled in a particular and historical way—in agreeing to the physical conception and birth of Jesus Christ—thereby becomes possible in spiritual terms for all human beings. As Elisabeth Behr-Sigel puts it, "Mary, the Mother of God, represents in her person this priesthood in communion with Christ, who, as the Letter to the Hebrews powerfully declares, is the one High Priest."[14]

[13]Bishop Kallistos of Diokleia, "Man, Woman and the Priesthood of Christ," in T. Hopko, ed., *Women and the Priesthood* (Crestwood, NY: St Vladimir's Seminary Press, 1999), 43–44.

[14]E. Behr Sigel, "The Ordination of Women: Also a Question for the Orthodox Churches", in E. Behr-Sigel and K. Ware, eds., *The Ordination of Women in the Orthodox Church* (Geneva: WCC, 2000), 41.

In moral terms, then, the Mother of God represents an example of human sanctity that is unsurpassed except by her Son. She embodies the ascetic ideal that was so fully embraced by the Church from the fourth century onward, but she also represents the archetypal "royal priesthood" of Christian believers. The Theotokos, by virtue of her holiness and moral integrity, thus becomes the meeting-place of the divine and created realms. There remains, however, another important aspect of Mary's virginity that, from the fifth century onward, began to dominate the liturgical celebration of her sanctity. This is the Christological meaning of the virgin birth, which the Fathers recognized as a sign of Christ's divinity, even as they continued to emphasize the physical reality of his Incarnation.

The Theotokos as Virgin: The Christological Dimension

From a theological point of view, the virginity of the Mother of God is of great significance. Christian writers recognized this from a very early period,[15] but the issue of Mary's virginal conception of Christ assumed prominence especially in the course of Christological discussions that took place in the first half of the fifth century. Theologians including Proclus of Constantinople and Cyril of Alexandria defended the doctrine that Mary contained the Son of God, or Word, in her womb from the moment of his conception. This position was upheld at the Council of Chalcedon in 451 and continued to be affirmed in liturgical texts thereafter.

---

[15]See, for example, Origen's *Commentary on John* 32.191: "If someone believes that [Christ] did not receive his birth from the Virgin Mary and the Holy Spirit, but from Joseph and Mary, he would be deficient in beliefs that are indispensible to possessing all faith." I am grateful to Peter Bouteneff for supplying me with this reference.

The following short hymn (*theotokion*) in praise of the Mother of God is a typical example:

> How should we not marvel at your Offspring, who is both God and man, all-honored one? For without knowing [a] man, O all-blameless, you gave birth in the flesh to a Son without father, begotten from the Father before the ages without mother, in no way undergoing change, or mixture or separation, but preserving intact the identity of either nature . . .[16]

The continuity of the Son of God, as Word and as Christ, the divine and human hypostasis, begotten eternally of the Father and born in history of Mary, is revealed in his virginal conception in her womb. As we have already seen, such purity forms part of a continuum in the life of the Theotokos—in both moral and physical terms—but it is as the paramount sign of God's entrance into creation *at the moment of his conception* that Mary's virginal state becomes most important.

Christ's virginal conception in the Mother of God reveals his eternal nature as Word and Son of God. As Nonna Verna Harrison has pointed out, the Fathers distinguished between two kinds of generation or origination. One, which applies only to divine existence, is the manner in which God the Father begets his Son, eternally and without any diminution of his own being. The Greek word that is used for this form of generation is γένεσις; this is usually translated as "generation" or "begetting" in order to convey the eternal and incorruptible nature of the process. The second kind of generation applies to creatures, including human beings,

---

[16]Trans. Archimandrite Ephrem Lash, Saturday Great Vespers, Tone 3, at <http://www.anastasis.org.uk/sat3ec.htm>.

who are born or created *ex nihilo*. The term that is applied to this process is γέννησις: it is closely related etymologically to γένεσις, but it refers to the origination of things or creatures in a material world that is subject to change, corruption and even death. The premise that lies behind such a distinction is that divine or spiritual reality transcends that with which we are familiar in the material world; whereas the former is eternal and stable, the latter is transient and subject to change.[17]

It is in the context of such reasoning that the miraculous and virginal conception of Christ takes on meaning. According to the Cappadocian Fathers, the divine and human Son of God was conceived and born of the Virgin Mary *in the same way* that he is generated eternally by the Father. In other words, his Incarnation involved a process that was not subject to the kind of corruption—or change—that is normally associated with human procreation. There are two aspects of such "corruption": one is that human birth-giving leads inevitably to the condition of all human beings, namely death; the other is that it involves sexual passion. Finally, and perhaps most importantly, the miraculous nature of Mary's birth-giving testified to Christ's eternal nature as the Word; if he had been conceived in the normal way, a new person would have come into existence in Mary's womb, rather than the eternal Son of God. The virginal conception and birth thus reveal Christ's divine and eternal nature even as he assumes the human nature that the Theotokos provides.

In addition to a concern for this continuity of person—the eternal divine Son of the Father and the Son born in time of Mary—there

---

[17]See N.V. Harrison, "Gender, Generation, and Virginity in Cappadocian Theology," *Journal of Theological Studies*, n.s. 47, Part 1 (1996), 38–68

is virginity's explicit link with divine and angelic forms of being. The Cappadocian Fathers, for example, believed that sexuality and procreation were unnecessary in the Garden of Eden and will become obsolete after the Final Resurrection, along with any kind of gender differentiation among human beings. In a striking passage in one of his poems, Gregory Nazianzen describes the holy Trinity as virginal in nature:

> The original virgin is the Holy Trinity. From the unoriginate Father came Christ the Lord, not having an external origin (for he himself is the Way and the Root and the Beginning of all things), nor again being born in the way that mortals are, but as Light coming forth from Light. From the Child, then, there is no other beloved child who makes a similar boast; so that the one remains the sole Parent, while the other is the sole Son, the most Unique from the Unique; these come together into one with the great Spirit, who comes likewise from the Father, one God opening up in threefold lights. Such is the Trinity's pure nature.[18]

As a feature of divine existence, virginity thus signifies incorruptibility and the promise of eternal life. Orthodox liturgical texts frequently allude to this connection, as we see in the Paschal Kanon of John of Damascus, in the troparion that follows the sixth ode:

> Having kept the seals intact, O Christ, you rose from the tomb, you who did not break the seal of the Virgin by your birth; and you have opened to us the gates of Paradise.[19]

[18]Gregory Nazianzen, *Carminum de Virginitate*, PG 37, cols. 523–24, lines 20–30, trans. Peter Gilbert; quoted in Harrison, "Gender, Generation, and Virginity," 51.

[19]*The Pentecostarion* (Boston, MA: Holy Transfiguration Monastery, 1990), 30 (with adjustments).

Christ, whose divine and human natures are revealed in his virginal birth, has restored eternal life to humanity by his own Resurrection.[20]

The Theotokos as Virgin: The Typological Dimension

As we saw in Chapter One, the Orthodox liturgical tradition frequently teaches this paradoxical doctrine by means of typology and poetic imagery, which appears in both homilies and hymns. This assumes that the mystery of Mary's birth-giving and Christ's Incarnation remains beyond human understanding. It is announced by the prophets, but is also hidden in suggestive signs that lurk throughout the Old Testament. It is worth exploring here a few of the main types, or signs, that are associated especially with the theme of Mary's virginity. I have already alluded to these in earlier chapters, but they deserve more detailed discussion here.

The bush that burned but was not consumed (Ex 3.1–8) is one of the best known types of the Mother of God. In its original context, this represents an important theophany in the Old Testament, when God appears to Moses and tells him to free the Jewish people from bondage in Israel. Gregory of Nyssa was the first Christian Father to associate this sign with Mary. He suggested that it foreshadows her virginal birth-giving, writing as follows in his *Life of Moses*:

> From this we learn also the mystery of the Virgin: the light of divinity which through birth shone from her into human

---

[20]E. Briere, "'Rejoice, Sceptre of Orthodoxy': Christology and the Mother of God," *Sobornost* 7.1 (1985), 18.

life did not consume the burning bush, even as the flower of her virginity was not withered by giving birth.[21]

Archimandrite Ephrem Lash comments that the Greek word that is used in the Septuagint for "bush" (βάτος) actually means "bramble."[22] When interpreted as a type of the Virgin Mary, this suggests her true humanity in all its thorny roughness. It is engulfed by fire, which represents divine power, but remains intact with "the flower of virginity," according to Gregory, continuing to bloom.

The gate of the temple that remained unopened is described in Ezekiel 43.27–44.4. This forms part of a prophecy concerning the gate that faced east and was shut. According to Ezekiel, an angel of the Lord declared to him, "This gate shall be shut; it shall not be opened, and no man shall enter by it, because the Lord God of Israel has entered by it; therefore it shall be shut." Christian commentators recognized in this prophecy a typological reference to the Mother of God. Like that temple gate, her virginal womb remained closed—except that the Son of God himself had passed through it. Some liturgical texts refer clearly to this type, as we see in a hymn sung in Matins on the feast of the Nativity of the Theotokos:

> She is the only gateway of the Only-begotten Son of God, who passed through this gate, yet kept it closed . . .[23]

[21]Gregory of Nyssa, *Life of Moses* 2.21, trans. A.J. Malherbe and E. Ferguson (New York, Ramsey and Toronto: Paulist Press, 1978), 59.

[22]Archimandrite Ephrem Lash, "Mary in Eastern Church Literature," in A. Stacpoole, ed., *Mary in Doctrine and Devotion* (Dublin: Columba Press, 1990), 68.

[23]Mother Mary and Archimandrite Kallistos Ware, trans., *The Festal Menaion* (London: Faber and Faber, 1969; repr. S. Canaan, PA: St Tikhon's Seminary

Other Old Testament types that refer specifically to Mary's virginity include the untouched garden, or paradise (Gen2.8–9), and the sealed spring or fountain of life (Ex 17.1–7 and Songs 4.12). The former sign, as we saw in the previous chapter, is associated with Irenaeus of Lyons' doctrine of recapitulation. The second-century theologian argued that Mary recapitulates, or re-enacts, not only the person and actions of Eve, but also the untouched garden from which God made the first Adam. In this way she is able to reverse the sequence of events that Genesis describes and to produce Christ, the Second Adam, who will bring God's plan of creation to fulfillment. The Song of Songs refers both backward to this garden and forward to the Virgin Mary, who will be "a spring shut up, a fountain sealed." Such imagery is pregnant with meaning: water is both the cause of natural life but also, if understood in a Christological sense, the source of eternal life, or in other words, Christ himself (Jn 4.14).

Festal hymns and homilies continuously employ such types, thereby emphasizing both the Christological message that is contained in both the Old and New Testaments and the extent to which Mary's role in the Incarnation was foretold. The Byzantine writers who composed the liturgical hymns that appear in the offices of the Marian feast-days do not usually explain the meaning of the types and prophecies to which they refer. It is assumed that the faithful will recognize their meaning, owing to

Press, 1998), 101. As Paul Ladouceur points out, however, some references to the Mother of God as "gate" may allude to another type, namely, Jacob's ladder (Gen 28.12–17). The meaning of the latter differs from Ezekiel's gate in that it presents Mary as the way that Christians may have access to God, rather than as the sealed repository of his divine presence. See P. Ladouceur, "Old Testament Prefigurations of the Mother of God," *St Vladimir's Theological Quarterly* 50, nos. 1–2 (2006), 43.

their long-standing place in liturgical tradition. The poetic significance of such types should also not be ignored: it is striking that Marian types such as the burning bush, the garden, and the spring are associated with creation. They remind Christians of Mary's role as a created being who conceived the Son of God in whom human and divine natures are hypostasized.

Such are a few of the typological signs that *foreshadow* the Christological mystery. The full extent of this mystery is beyond human comprehension or logical expression. Christ, who remained fully eternal while assuming human nature at his conception, transcended the normal rules of physical reproduction. Mary, the Theotokos, or "God-bearer," remained throughout this process and for the rest of her life a pure, virginal human being of both physical and moral integrity. It is the focus on that world-changing moment of the conception, however, that causes Mary's virginity to assume such importance in this mystery. This represents the foundation for all Orthodox Christian reflection on the Theotokos, which emphasizes her purity above all in connection with her role in the Incarnation of Christ.

Conclusion

The virginity of Mary, the Mother of God, thus plays an essential role in the mystery of the Incarnation of Christ, the Word of God. It can be interpreted in both moral and theological ways in Orthodox Christian tradition—and of course these two aspects of her purity are intertwined. It is important to recognize, however, that this blessed state does not distance Mary entirely from the rest of humanity. Theological treatises, liturgical texts, sermons, and hagiography all stress—sometimes by means of typology rather than discursively—the fact that the Theotokos is rooted in creation. She represents, however, creation as God intended it to be: it is full of joy, hope, and fertile promise. Such a creation, or "virgin earth," as Irenaeus calls it,[24] is capable of bringing forth Jesus Christ, the Second Adam, who will grant the world salvation and eternal life. This had to occur through and by means of a created but undefiled human being, the Virgin Mary and all-holy Birth-giver of God.

Further Reading:

Brakke, David. *Athanasius and Asceticism*. Baltimore and London: Johns Hopkins University Press, 1995.

Brown, Peter. *The Body and Society: Men, Women and Sexual Renunciation in Early Christianity*. New York: Columbia University Press, 1988.

Foskett, Mary F. *A Virgin Conceived. Mary and Classical Representations of Virginity*. Bloomington and Indianapolis: Indiana University Press, 2002.

Gabriel, George S. *Mary: The Untrodden Portal of God* (esp. Chap. 3: "Ever-Virginity"). Ridgewood, NJ: Zephyr Publishing 2000; rev. ed. 2005.

Harrison, Verna E.F. "Gender, Generation, and Virginity in Cappadocian Theology." *Journal of Theological Studies*, n.s. 47, Part 1 (1996), 38–68.

---

[24]Irenaeus of Lyons, *On the Apostolic Preaching* I. 32, trans. J. Behr (Crestwood, NY: St Vladimir's Seminary Press, 1997), 61.

chapter five

"THE THEOTOKOS": MARY'S PLACE IN CHRISTOLOGICAL DOCTRINE

In addressing the Virgin Mary as "Mother of God," Orthodox Christians express, in just one short phrase, her theological importance in the Christian dispensation. The Mother of God contained in her womb Christ, the Word of God, who is uncontained by the whole of creation. The eighth-century preacher and theologian, St John of Damascus, describes this mystery in a sermon on the Nativity of the Mother of God, as follows:

> He who has an eternal Father was borne in the womb by you! O earth-born little daughter who carried the Creator in your God-bearing arms!

This statement expresses the doctrine of the "double birth" to which we alluded in the previous chapter, namely, that the same Son who is begotten eternally by the Father is the One who is born of the Theotokos. John also summarizes here the paradox that is embodied in Mary, the Mother of God. She conceived and bore Christ the Word and gave birth to him while remaining herself an "earth-born little daughter." Later in the same homily,

John emphasizes even more explicitly the fact that Christ took his human nature from Mary:

> For from you alone the Maker received a share, that is, the first-fruit of our dough. For his flesh is from your flesh, and his blood is from your blood, and God suckled milk from your breasts, and your lips were united with the lips of God. O incomprehensible and ineffable matters![1]

The extraordinary nature of this paradox reflects the ontological gulf between God and his creation. Jesus Christ, the Word of God, is our Maker; he is eternal and all things, including humankind, depend on him for their existence. And yet, as we see in the second passage of John of Damascus's sermon, this Creator God took human flesh from the Virgin Mary and nursed at her breast. *From her flesh alone*, Christ became incarnate and joined the human race. In this way, Mary acted as a link between the divine and the created states of being. As we have already seen in previous chapters, Orthodox liturgical texts use many types and metaphors to express this mysterious role for Mary, including "bridge," "ladder," and "temple."

The Greek Fathers employed two main epithets to express Mary's role as "Mother of God." The earliest of the two epithets is "Theotokos" (Θεοτόκος), which means literally "God-bearer" or "Birthgiver of God." This term began to be used frequently by Christian writers, including Alexander of Alexandria, Eusebius of Caesarea, Athanasius, and the Cappadocian Fathers, from the early fourth

---

[1]Both passages are translated in M.B. Cunningham, *Wider Than Heaven: Eighth-Century Homilies on the Mother of God* (Crestwood, NY: St Vladimir's Seminary Press, 2008), 63.

century onward.[2] The epithet conveys above all a Christological message: it reminds us that Mary bore and gave birth to the Divine Son. In Greek, "Theo-" derives from the noun "Theos" for God; "-tokos" comes from a root of the verb "tikto," meaning "to give birth." The second epithet, "Mētēr Theou" (Μήτηρ Θεοῦ), which literally means "Mother of God," appeared from approximately the sixth century onward in Byzantine liturgical texts. At first the term seems to have been used interchangeably with "Theotokos," expressing Mary's role in the mystery of the Incarnation. In the sixth century, however, Romanos the Melodist portrayed Mary for the first time as a person with strong maternal feelings for her son, Jesus Christ. Later Byzantine preachers and hymnographers, from about the eighth century onward, developed this idea further. We see it, for example, in the sermon by John of Damascus that was quoted above, when the preacher describes Mary nursing and kissing the infant Christ. Modern English translations of liturgical texts tend to translate both "Theotokos" and "Mētēr Theou" as "Mother of God." In a sense, this is allowable since the terms "Bearer" and "Birth-giver" of God are not used in colloquial speech and may thus be viewed by some English speakers as meaningless. However, it is important to remember that the original Greek versions of these texts convey different nuances in their choice of the names "Theotokos" or "Mētēr Theou" for Mary. Whereas the former may have been chosen to convey above all her theological role in the Incarnation, the latter (especially in later Byzantine texts) may allude to her maternal relationship with Christ.

[2]For a list of these sources, see John McGuckin, *St Cyril of Alexandria and the Christological Controversy* (Crestwood, NY: St Vladimir's Seminary Press, 2004), 22, n. 52. Earlier Fathers, such as Origen, may have used the term "Theotokos" occasionally, but it became more common in theological texts of the fourth century.

In this chapter we will focus primarily on the Christological meaning of Mary's role as "Theotokos." The more personal aspects of her place as "Mētēr Theou" will be taken up in Chapter Five, on intercession, in which we will explore Mary's relationship, as *mother*, to both Christ and, in a metaphorical sense, to the Church. Both of Mary's roles are stressed in Orthodox tradition, often interchangeably, not only in the liturgical texts that make up the divine offices, but also in icons and other holy objects. As we saw above, it was Mary's Christological importance (in a theological sense) that received emphasis first, from as early as the second but especially from the fourth century onward. To the extent that this could be discerned, on the basis of Scripture and tradition, early Christian writers needed to understand how the Incarnation took place and what its implications were for humanity and the whole of creation. Sometimes such speculation took place against a background of controversy with external critics of the Church, such as Jews, pagans, or Gnostics; sometimes it evolved in the context of discussion—or even controversy—within Christian communities.

After looking first at the fifth-century debate concerning Christ's humanity and divinity, especially with regard to the Virgin Mary's role in the Incarnation, we will explore how later Christian writers expressed this by means of poetic imagery and typology. This, as we have been seeing throughout this book, is the form of theological teaching about the Mother of God that is most familiar to Orthodox Christians since it pervades the prayers and hymnography of the Church. It expresses in an allusive but unequivocal way the mystery of God's entrance into his own creation through the womb of a pure, but entirely human, young woman named Mary.

The Epithet "Theotokos" and Fifth-Century Christological Debate

The fourth-century Fathers who referred to the Virgin Mary as "Theotokos" were fully aware of the theological implications of this term. In his treatise, *On the Incarnation*, for example, Athanasius of Alexandria writes about this mystery in the following way:

> [Christ] formed his own body from the Virgin; and that is no small proof of his divinity, since he who made that was the Maker of all else. And would not anyone infer from the fact of that body being begotten of a Virgin only, without human father, that he who appeared in it was also Maker and Lord of all beside?[3]

Athanasius stresses Christ's simultaneous humanity and divinity in this passage, citing Mary's virginity as proof of the latter. Elsewhere in the same treatise, he describes the Virgin's body as a "temple," which Christ sanctified by his sojourn there.[4]

Gregory of Nazianzus, building on the Alexandrian understanding of the Incarnation of Christ, the Word of God, from the moment of his conception, famously declared:

> If anyone does not admit that holy Mary is Birth-giver of God (Theotokos), he is cut off from the Godhead. If anyone claims that Christ merely passed through Mary, as if passing

---

[3]Athanasius, *On the Incarnation* 18, trans. A Religious of the C.S.M.V., *St Athanasius on the Incarnation* (London and Oxford: Mowbray, rev. ed. 1953), 47 (with adjustments).

[4]Athanasius, *On the Incarnation* 9 and 17, trans. A Religious of the C.S.M.V., *St Athanasius on the Incarnation*, 34 and 46.

---

through a channel, but denies that he was formed within her in a divine way (because there was no intervention of a man), and in a human way (that is, according to the laws of conception), he is equally godless. If anyone says that a man was formed first, who only afterward was clothed with divinity, let him be condemned . . .[5]

It is clear from this passage that Gregory did not question Orthodox acceptance of the title "Theotokos" for the Virgin Mary; in fact he insisted upon it. In addition to conveying the honor that is due to her owing to her role as Christ's mother, the term was for him an essential element in Christological understanding. Such a view remained unquestioned until the beginning of the fifth century, when the patriarch Nestorius suddenly took exception to its widespread use in Christian discourse.

Nestorius was elected to the episcopal throne of the imperial city, Constantinople, in 428, having been trained in a monastery near Antioch in Syria. He had already gained a strong reputation in his native land as both preacher and ascetic. Almost immediately after his ordination, Nestorius adopted a vigorous policy of eliminating heresy in the Church and exhorting the faithful to be more pious and austere in their way of life. In addition to this, Nestorius and his deputy, a priest named Anastasius, began to preach against the use of the epithet "Theotokos" for the Virgin Mary.

Why, we may ask, did Nestorius object so strongly to the term "Theotokos," which had been used for so long to describe the mystery of Mary's motherhood of Christ, the Incarnate Word?

[5]*Letter 101 to Cledonius*, trans. L. Gambero, *Mary and the Fathers of the Church. The Blessed Virgin Mary in Patristic Thought* (San Francisco: Ignatius Press, 1999), 162 (with adjustments).

The answer is not easy to determine. Historical accounts of the affair are subjective and some date from decades after the event. Many of Nestorius's own writings have been destroyed, owing to the fact that he was condemned three years later at the council of Ephesus. However, enough of the correspondence between Nestorius and his main critic, Cyril, bishop of Alexandria, survives for us to reconstruct where their theological differences lay.

It is also clear that politics played a part in the dispute. Some historians have stressed the importance of power struggles between the episcopal sees of Alexandria, Antioch and Constantinople, as well as the interplay of strong personalities, including not only Nestorius and Cyril of Alexandria, but also the empress Pulcheria and the Constantinopolitan court.[6] For our purposes, it is the theological aspects of the controversy that are significant. In addition, and as Richard Price has convincingly argued, this controversy was primarily Christological.[7] Although the dispute had implications for the veneration of Mary the Theotokos, it was concerned above all with the need to arrive at a correct understanding of the way in which the human and divine natures come together in Christ.

[6]For such an approach to the problem, see, for example, K. Holum, *Theodosian Empresses: Women and Imperial Dominion in Late Antiquity* (Berkeley, CA: University of California Press, 1982); K. Cooper, "Contesting the Nativity: Wives, Virgins, and Pulcheria's *Imitatio Mariae,"* *Scottish Journal of Religious Studies* 19.1 (1998), 31–43.

[7]See R. Price, "Marian Piety and the Nestorian Controversy," in R.N. Swanson, ed., *The Church and Mary,* Studies in Church History 39 (Woodbridge, Suffolk: Boydell Press, 2004), 31–8; idem, "The Theotokos and the Council of Ephesus", in Chris Maunder, ed., *The Origins of the Cult of the Virgin Mary* (London and New York: Burns & Oates, Continuum, 2008), 89–103.

Soon after his election as patriarch, Nestorius instituted a series of public lectures in the Great Church of Constantinople in order to explore the role of the Virgin Mary in the Incarnation of Christ. His assistant presbyter, Anastasius, opened with a sermon in which he criticized the use of the "Theotokos" epithet for the Virgin Mary. According to the historian Socrates (c. 380–450), he argued, "Let no man call Mary 'Theotokos' for she was but a woman, and it is impossible for God to be born of a woman."[8] In response to this sermon, another bishop named Proclus, who was living in Constantinople at this time, preached a sermon on the Incarnation that emphasized the essential role that Mary, the Theotokos, played in this event.[9]

A series of public protests and letters followed the events of Nestorius's first year in office. In Constantinople, both monks and secular leaders began to demonstrate openly against the policies of the archbishop. Eventually, news filtered out of Constantinople and reached the ears of the archbishop of Alexandria, Cyril. He began to send letters—protesting against Nestorius's theological views—to monks in Egypt, the papacy in Rome, and Nestorius himself. Nestorius responded robustly, but also began to petition the emperor for an ecumenical council, which he hoped would settle the matter, once and for all.

The council eventually took place in Ephesus during the summer of 431 with about 200 bishops in attendance. Unfortunately, however, the delegation of bishops from Antioch, along with

---

[8]Socrates, *Ecclesiastical History* 7.32, trans. J. Stevenson, *Creeds, Councils and Controversies. Documents Illustrating the History of the Church, AD 337–461* (London: SPCK, rev ed. 1989), 288.

[9]Constas, *Proclus of Constantinople*, 135.

those from Rome, were delayed on their journeys and thus not included in the deliberations. It is not surprising that Cyril of Alexandria, backed by his supporters, won the support of the council. It ended by anathematizing Nestorius and his teachings on the grounds that his theology undermined the union of God and man in Jesus Christ.[10]

As we consider the consequences of the council of Ephesus, which included the departure of Nestorius from his see in Constantinople, his embittered exile in Egypt, and the formation of the Assyrian Church of the East (which remains out of communion with the Chalcedonian and non-Chalcedonian Churches to this day),[11] it is possible, as some modern commentators have done, to consider this as one more example of the kind of misunderstanding that a clash of incompatible personalities can cause within the Church. Such a view would argue that the Christological positions of Cyril, Nestorius, and their supporters were not in fact so very far apart: tragically, they ended up exaggerating and misrepresenting each others' views, forcing the debate into two

[10]The story is actually more complicated than this, but I have simplified it for the sake of brevity. Following a second—much smaller—council that was convened by the Syrian party, which in turn anathematized Cyril of Alexandria and his teachings, the emperor Theodosius II deposed not only Nestorius, but also Cyril and Memnon, the bishop of Ephesus. He decided about two years later to reinstate the latter two figures, but Nestorius remained in exile where he later wrote in defence of his doctrinal position. For the full narrative of these tragic events, see McGuckin, *Saint Cyril of Alexandria*, 20–125; Young, *From Nicaea to Chalcedon*, 213–65.

[11]This has also come to be known (incorrectly) as the 'Nestorian' Church. Although it is certainly true that it was formed as a direct result of Nestorius's condemnation at the council of Ephesus, it also follows the teachings of other great Antiochene teachers, such as Theodore of Mopsuestia.

opposing positions. There is certainly some truth to this view and, we may speculate, if Cyril and Nestorius had been more willing to understand each other's positions, the schism might never have taken place.

However, it is also fair to say that this debate developed because real differences exist between the two Christological positions. An important aspect of this doctrine, for both Nestorius and Cyril, was the proper understanding of the role of the Theotokos in the Incarnation. Christ took on flesh and became incarnate in Mary's womb. For Cyril, this meant that the Theotokos conceived and gave birth to Christ the Logos, while for Nestorius, it ensured his truly human Incarnation. With hindsight, we can see that each of these views has theological merit; for the protagonists, greater emphasis had to be placed on one or the other, rather than on both. In order to understand them more fully, it is necessary first to look at the intellectual backgrounds that influenced Nestorius and Cyril, and secondly, to attempt to understand their individual interpretations of Mary's role in the Incarnation.

Nestorius was influenced by a method of biblical exegesis (often associated with—but by no means confined to—a Syrian milieu) that stressed the historical truth of the Bible and to the reality of Christ's human Incarnation. Following such Syrian theologians as Theodoret of Cyrrhus and Theodore of Mopsuestia, Nestorius accepted three ways of interpreting Scripture: literal, moral, and allegorical. He tended to prioritize the first of these on the grounds that it is God's dispensation, as acted out in history, that will lead to human salvation. This history culminated in the Incarnation of Christ, when the Son or Word of God joined himself with a human being and became the incarnate Jesus Christ. Cyril of Alexandria meanwhile followed a tradition of biblical exegesis that is usually associated with that great city in Egypt. Following the teachings of Philo (a first-century Jewish philosopher), Clement, Origen, Athanasius and others, the fifth-century bishop favoured a more allegorical interpretation of Scripture. This position had become associated, especially in the course of the fourth century, with an emphasis on Christ's eternal nature as Word of God, which was in no way compromised by his conception and Incarnation.

In formulating his ideas about how divinity and humanity come together in the Son of God, Nestorius thus focused on the historical narrative that the Gospels provide. Jesus Christ truly lived and taught in first-century Judaea, being born of a woman (Gal 4.4) and dying on the cross. The Gospels bear witness to the Lord's true humanity, which enabled him to live among human beings and to re-orientate their lives towards God. In spite of this emphasis on the historical reality of Jesus's life and death, Nestorius also subscribed fully to the definitions of the first two ecumenical councils, which state that Christ is fully divine, consubstantial (*homoousios*) and co-eternal with the Father. He was not, as his contemporaries falsely accused him of being, a believer in the doctrine that Christ was simply an "inspired man."[12]

Nestorius's main worry, as revealed in his objection to the epithet "Theotokos" for the Virgin Mary, was that the Alexandrians were in danger of confusing, or mixing, the two natures that came together in Christ. Since divinity, as the stronger and higher state of existence, is likely to subsume the human nature, Nestorius was

[12]Nestorius was accused of following the heresy of Paul of Samosata, who taught that the divine Logos 'indwelt' a human person, Jesus, in order to provide him with divine inspiration. See McGuckin, *St Cyril of Alexandria*, 28.

afraid that in insisting on their complete union in the incarnate Christ, the Alexandrians risked falling into the heresy of Apollinarianism, that is, the belief that the divine Logos took the place of a human soul. It is for this reason that Nestorius insisted that the two natures remain distinct and separate. Christ, he believed, acted sometimes in his role as God (as for example when he worked miracles) but at other times experienced the whole range of human emotions, suffering, and death. Nestorius's main objection to the epithet "Theotokos" for the Virgin Mary, then, was that it only emphasizes Christ's divine nature. A more appropriate epithet, he suggested, would be "Christotokos" or "Birth-giver of Christ," the incarnate Lord who is both divine *and* human. Connected with this view, and important for our study of the Virgin Mary, is the belief that she played only a limited role in helping to bring about the Incarnation of Christ. She certainly contributed to his human nature in conceiving and giving birth to him, but she had no contact with his divine nature. Indeed, Nestorius seems to have argued that this nature began to be manifested fully only after Christ grew to maturity and was baptized.[13]

Meanwhile Cyril of Alexandria, who was indebted to the Trinitarian theology that had been developed by fourth-century predecessors such as Athanasius, developed a Christological position that expressed the complete union of divinity and humanity in Christ. According to Cyril, Jesus Christ was fully God and man from the moment of his conception. Mary, the Theotokos, bore and gave birth to the incarnate Word of God. Whereas Nestorius's supporters had developed a simple slogan, "in (*en*) two natures,"

[13]F. Loofs, *Nestorius and His Place in the History of Christian Doctrine* (Cambridge: Cambridge University Press, 1914; repr. Elibron Classics, 2005), 83–6.

to express their understanding of Christ's person, Cyril preferred the formula, "unity out of (*ek*) two natures." To give a concrete example of how these two theologies function, we may use the story of the raising of Lazarus (Jn 11). In his exegesis of this passage, Nestorius would emphasize the way in which it reveals both the human and the divine natures of Christ: thus he would point to the way that Christ wept, as a human being, at the death of his friend but then, as God, raised him from the dead. Cyril of Alexandria, meanwhile, would argue that Christ knew from the very beginning that Lazarus would be resurrected; he wept in order to teach his disciples and the Jews that he truly loved this man. Cyril saw that Nestorius's theology presents a problem with regard to Jesus Christ's subjectivity: this incarnate God-man appears, according to Nestorius, to be a split personality, acting divinely at one moment and in a completely human manner at another.

The implications of Cyril's Christology with regard to Mary are immediately apparent: not only should she be called "Theotokos," but she should herself be venerated since she conceived, carried, and bore Christ the Word and Son of God. Cyril writes in his *Five Tomes Against Nestorius*, composed during the spring of 430 in response to the series of public lectures that the latter had organized, as follows:

> Tell me, therefore, why do you begrudge such a title to the holy Virgin, and moreover deprive her of the dignity of divine birth and say that she is not "Theotokos"?[14]

For Cyril, Mary is the "venerable treasure of the entire world, inextinguishable lamp, crown of virginity, scepter of Orthodoxy,

[14]Trans. Norman Russell, *Cyril of Alexandria* (London & New York: Routledge, 2000), 137.

imperishable temple, container of him who cannot be contained, Mother and Virgin . . ."[15] While this language may seem extravagant, we should note that in all of his writings, Cyril frames his discussions of the Virgin Mary in a Christological context. He does not stress her stature as a holy figure except insofar as she gave birth to God. Many of Cyril's writings on this topic are polemical, however, which influences how he expresses himself. Like many other Christians in this period, he felt a strong attachment to the Mother of God, not only for her conception and birthgiving of Christ but also because of her embodiment of Christian virtue and faith.

In summary, it is clear that the Theotokos issue was just one aspect—albeit a very important one—of the wider Christological debate that was taking place in the first half of the fifth century. It is the epithet itself that seems to have sparked off this debate, but it remained primarily a Christological issue, not a Marian one. After the condemnation of Nestorius and his theology at the council of Ephesus in 431, it was the Alexandrian Christological position that prevailed. However, this was considerably modified in the decades that followed, as a result of dialogues between Cyril and his followers, bishops of Antioch, and Pope Leo I. The Christological definition that was agreed upon at the council of Chalcedon in 451 strove to perfect two theological positions that had—in the course of the twenty years since the council of Ephesus—themselves been modified in significant ways.

---

[15]This phrase appears in Cyril's Homily 4, which he is said to have delivered at Ephesus in the course of the council. Trans. Gambero, *Mary and the Fathers of the Church*, 247.

The Expression of a Mystery:
Imagery, Typology and Paradox

Mary's role in the Incarnation of Christ is often described in Orthodox liturgical texts by means of poetic imagery and typology. As we have seen throughout this book, such a manner of expressing this fundamental truth is especially characteristic of Orthodox Christianity: it is evocative, but also perhaps puzzling for those who are unfamiliar with such symbolic language. Why did liturgical writers, from about the fifth century onward, choose to teach Christian doctrine in this way? Perhaps the answer to this question is related to the silence with which New Testament writers treated Mary's role as Christ's mother and disciple. She inhabits a paradox that remains ineffable and mysterious. In the discussion that follows, we shall explore the meaning of some of the images of the Mother of God that appear in Orthodox liturgical texts. As we shall see, these express in different ways the mystery that lies at the heart of Christian doctrine.

One of the earliest writers to expand the poetic and typological vocabulary of the Incarnation, and the role that Mary played in it, was the fifth-century bishop, Proclus of Constantinople. As we saw earlier, Proclus was involved in the Christological debate that developed in the Constantinopolitan patriarchate after Nestorius's arrival as archbishop in 428. The sermon that Proclus preached, probably on December 26, a day that had recently been dedicated to the memory of the Mother of God, is a masterpiece of oratorical eloquence. Proclus explores here a range of poetic images that express Mary's role as "container of God," "place" where the Incarnation occurred, and "workshop" where the divine and human natures came together in Christ. In the prologue of the homily, Proclus writes, for example:

> She who called us here today is the Holy Mary; the untarnished vessel of virginity; the spiritual paradise of the second Adam (cf. Rom 5.14); the workshop for the union of natures; the market-place of the contract of salvation; the bridal chamber in which the Word took the flesh in marriage . . .[16]

Proclus's use of metaphors that evoke natural objects, such as "vessel," "market-place," and so on, is deliberate. He is emphasizing Mary's humanity, even if she is also pure and holy. The mystery lies in the fact that the fully Divine Son of God himself, who is uncontainable and transcendent, came to dwell in her womb. Thus, the divine and created spheres of existence were joined together in a wholly new and paradoxical way. One of Proclus's most memorable images is that of the "loom." He pictures Mary as the "awesome loom of the divine economy" on which the "robe of union" (that is, the Incarnation) was woven, with detailed attention to the roles of each participant:

> The loom-worker was the Holy Spirit; the wool-worker was the overshadowing power from on high (cf. Lk 1.35). The wool was the ancient fleece of Adam; the interlocking thread the spotless flesh of the Virgin. The weaver's shuttle was propelled by the immeasurable grace of him who wore the robe; the artisan was the Word who entered in through her sense of hearing.[17]

---

[16]Proclus of Constantinople, Homily 1.1, trans. N. Constas, *Proclus of Constantinople and the Cult of the Virgin in Late Antiquity. Homilies 1–5, Texts and Translations* (Leiden: Brill, 2003), 137.

[17]Homily 1.1, trans. Constas, *Proclus of Constantinople*, 137. See also Constas's interesting analysis of this homily in his article, "Weaving the Body of God: Proclus of Constantinople, the Theotokos, and the Loom of the Flesh", *Journal of Early Christian Studies* 3.2 (1995), 169–94.

Another early liturgical text, which employs many different metaphors for the Mother of God's place in the mystery of the Incarnation, is the *Akathistos Hymn*.[18] The imagery that is used in this liturgical text, like that in Proclus's homilies, frequently describes the Virgin Mary as the vehicle for, or container of, the Incarnation. She is the "celestial ladder by which God descended," "bridge leading those from earth to heaven," and "dwelling-place for him who is above the Seraphim."[19] As in the case of Proclus's poetry, some of these passages evoke passages in Scripture, including both the Old and the New Testaments, whereas others seem to act purely as metaphors recalling the natural world or everyday life. From a theological point of view, the latter remind Christians of the physical reality of Christ's Incarnation: he took human nature from a woman who was firmly rooted in creation and who could thus be identified as "earth," "tree," "wood," and so on.[20] In many cases, biblical references and metaphor overlap, as in the case of "earth," which evokes the untilled earth from which the first Adam was formed (Gen 2.7). So why use metaphor, instead of attempting to describe Mary's place in the Incarnation in more prosaic terms? The answer lies in the profundity of the subject. Early liturgical writers, including Proclus and the author of the *Akathistos Hymn*, perceived that Mary's birth-giving role cannot be explained by means of logic: the best way to deepen our apprehension of the mystery is to evoke parallels in the natural world.

[18]See Chapter Three, pp. 82–84.

[19]*The Akathistos Hymn*, trans. L.M. Peltomaa, *The Image of the Virgin Mary in the Akathistos Hymn* (Leiden: Brill, 2001), 3–19.

[20]*The Akathistos Hymn* 5 and 13, trans. Peltomaa, *The Image of the Virgin Mary*, 7 and 13.

Closely related to poetic imagery and metaphor, and often over-lapping with it, is typology. As we have seen throughout this book, typology is the study of Old Testament events, people, or objects that point towards the salvation that will arrive in the new dispensation. Individual types, such as Jacob's ladder (Gen 28.10–17) and the burning bush (Ex 3.1–8) express the mystery of the Incarnation of Christ in different ways. Those that are associated with the holy places that contained God, according to the old dispensation, precisely foreshadow Mary's role as Theotokos. She is described as "tabernacle," "holy of holies," "table" (on which the bread of life reposes), "jar," and other objects associated with the worship of the old Covenant.[21] We are reminded that Mary, the Theotokos, supersedes these holy containers by acting as a *living* receptacle for the incarnate Son of God.

Another evocative type for the Mother of God, which appears frequently in hymns and homilies, is that of "Gideon's fleece" (Judg 6.37–40). Although the connection between a sign that God granted Gideon, in order to prove his protection of him in the battle against the Midianites, and the Virgin Mary may not be immediately obvious, this type, like that of Jacob's ladder, revealed for the Fathers the manner in which God would later enter his creation as the incarnate Christ. John Chrysostom interprets the "dew on the fleece" as a sign of the way in which Christ "noiselessly and gently entered into the Virgin's womb."[22]

---

[21]Paul Ladouceur, "Old Testament Prefigurations of the Mother of God," *St Vladimir's Theological Quarterly* 50, nos. 1–2 (2006), 10.

[22]John Chrysostom, *Homily on Matthew* 26.39.3, cited and trans. Ladouceur, "Old Testament Prefigurations of the Mother of God," 25.

Some types, such as the "light breeze" of 3 Kingdoms 19.12 (LXX) or the "shaded mountain" of Habakkuk 3.3, are more enigmatic in meaning. It is sometimes necessary to recall the entire passage and to meditate on its significance in order to perceive how it relates to the Mother of God. Sometimes such types evoke parallel examples: in the case of the shaded mountain, we are reminded of other mountains that prefigured Virgin Mary, including those featuring in Exodus 19–20, Daniel 2.34, and Isaiah 2.2. While each of these types signifies above all Mary's role as container of God, their poetic evocation of her connection with nature is unmistakable. The Virgin Mary represents the place where God enters his material creation; she is the point of contact between two, ontologically distinct, modes of being. Such signs also reinforce, by poetic means, Mary's true humanity and ongoing link with the rest of creation.

Conclusions

Finally, it is worth reiterating the reason why allusions to Mary—whether these are theoretical, poetic, or typological—are so pervasive in Orthodox Christian theology. This is because Mary, the Theotokos or Mother of God, plays an essential role in the divine dispensation. As so many of the Church's liturgical texts indicate, Mary represents the link between God and his creation. Her physical nature, which images and types such as "earth" or "mountain" recall, is never abandoned, even when she becomes the Bearer and Mother of God. It is true that, especially after the reinstatement of Cyrilline Christology in Byzantine thought after about the sixth century, Mary's role as "Mother of God" began to be reflected in her growing stature as a holy figure in her own right.[23] However, Orthodox theologians, liturgical writers, and iconographers have never lost sight of the Virgin's humanity, which anchors her in the created world and assures her role as merciful intercessor for all Christians.

Further Reading:

Constas, Nicholas. *Proclus of Constantinople and the Cult of the Virgin in Late Antiquity. Homilies 1–5, Texts and Translations.* Leiden and Boston: Brill, 2003.

Cunningham, Mary B. "The Meeting of the Old and the New: The Typology of Mary the Theotokos in Byzantine Homilies and Hymns," in R.N. Swanson, ed., *The Church and Mary. Studies in Church History* 39. Woodbridge, Suffolk: Boydell and Brewster, 2004, 52–62.

Lash, Archimandrite Ephrem. "Mary in Eastern Church Literature," in A. Stacpoole, OSB, ed., *Mary in Doctrine and Devotion.* Dublin: Columba Press, 1990, 58–80.

McGuckin, John. *Saint Cyril of Alexandria and the Christological Controversy: Its History, Theology and Texts.* Crestwood, NY: St Vladimir's Seminary Press, 2004.

Price, Richard. "Theotokos: The Title and Its Significance in Doctrine and Devotion," in Sarah Boss, ed., *Mary: The Complete Resource.* London and New York: Continuum, 2007, 56–73.

Young, Frances M. *From Nicaea to Chalcedon: A Guide to the Literature and Its Background.* London: SCM Press, 1983.

---

[23]For discussion of this theory, see especially Price, "Theotokos: The Title and Its Significance in Doctrine and Devotion," in Sarah Boss, ed., *Mary: The Complete Resource* (London and New York: Continuum), 65–9.

chapter six

"IMMOVABLE TOWER OF THE CHURCH": THE MOTHER OF GOD AS INTERCESSOR

The important role that Mary, the Theotokos, plays in the Christological mystery leads naturally to her veneration by Orthodox Christians. While Mary's human nature makes her accessible to the faithful as an intercessor before God, her association with Christ, the divine Son, ensures her position of power and influence. Many liturgical texts weave together the Christological message concerning the Mother of God with invocation of her intercessory role. This can be illustrated by the following short hymn, or theotokion, that is sung in Vespers on the Sunday of the Last Judgment, just before the beginning of Lent:

> The heavenly powers praise thee, O Virgin Mother full of grace, and we also glorify thy childbearing that none can understand. O Theotokos, pray for the salvation of our souls.[1]

In the first section of the hymn, we are reminded of Mary's virginity and role as Birth-giver of Christ. After this, however, the

[1]Mother Mary and Archimandrite Kallistos Ware, trans., *The Lenten Triodion* (London: Faber and Faber, 1978; repr. South Canaan, PA: St Tikhon's Seminary Press, 2002), 167.

hymnographer calls on the Mother of God as intercessor; she is asked to pray for the salvation of the Christian faithful.

Whereas Christian writers recognized the central role that the Virgin Mary played in the Incarnation of Christ from an early date, as we have seen in the last two chapters, the evidence for devotion to her as a holy figure was slower to develop. We will trace this process—to the extent that it can be discerned—in the first section of this chapter, before going on to explore the more abundant evidence for devotion to the Mother of God from about the late sixth century onward. She defended the imperial city of Constantinople from its enemies and was later adopted as the patron and protector of the monasteries on Mt Athos. This position was upheld in both the public (or official) and the private spheres. Many texts and artifacts suggest that Byzantine Christians at every social or political level regarded the Virgin Mary as their primary intercessor. Such honor and veneration continues to the present day: while remaining a symbol of the Incarnation, Mary also acts as a major intermediary in Orthodox Christian supplication to God.

The Emergence of Devotion towards the Virgin Mary as Intercessor

Although the Virgin Mary received honor as Christ's mother during the first three Christian centuries, she does not appear to have assumed an active intercessory role, as early martyrs like St Thekla did, until somewhat later.[2] Relics, shrines, and miracle sto-

---

[2]For a summary of this question, see S. Shoemaker, "The Cult of the Virgin in the Fourth Century: A Fresh Look at Some Old and New Sources," in C. Maunder, ed., *The Origins of the Cult of the Virgin Mary* (New York

ries relating to the Mother of God begin to be attested frequently only in about the middle of the fifth century.[3] A premonition of the important role that Mary would later assume for Christians does appear, however, in Irenaeus of Lyon's *Against Heresies*, written at the end of the second century. Irenaeus describes her as Eve's "advocate" (παράκλητος) since she reversed the latter's act of disobedience and reconciled her to God.[4] This is a word that is used both in the New Testament (cf. Jn 16.7) and in later liturgical texts for the Holy Spirit; it may also be translated as "intercessor" or "comforter" and is based (in Greek) on the idea of invocation, or the calling down, of divine grace.

Further evidence of growing belief in the Virgin Mary's intercessory power may be found in a papyrus fragment that most scholars place no later than the second half of the fourth century, though some believe it may be earlier.[5] The papyrus contains a short prayer addressed to the Virgin, which is usually given the Latin title, "Sub tuum praesidium." The Greek text reads (in translation) as follows:

and London: Burns and Oates / Continuum, 2008), 71–2; on St Thekla, see Stephen Davis, *The Cult of St Thecla* (Oxford: Oxford University Press, 2001).

[3]For the sites in Jerusalem, see S.J. Shoemaker, *Ancient Traditions of the Virgin Mary's Dormition and Assumption* (Oxford: Oxford University Press, 2002), 78–141; for Constantinople, see J. Wortley, "The Marian Relics at Constantinople," *Greek, Roman and Byzantine Studies* 45 (2005), 171–87.

[4]Irenaeus, *Against the Heresies* V.19.1, ANF, vol. 1, 547. See also the discussion above, Chapter Three, pp. 76–7.

[5]Shoemaker, "Marian Liturgies," 130; R.M. Price, "The Theotokos and the Council of Ephesus," in C. Maunder, ed., *The Origins of the Cult of the Virgin Mary* (London and New York: Continuum, 2008), 89.

We take refuge in your compassion, Theotokos. Do not disregard our prayers in troubling times, but deliver us from danger, O only pure one, only blessed one.[6]

The title "Theotokos" ("Birth-giver of God") should not surprise us; as we saw in the previous chapter, theological writers were addressing the Virgin Mary by this name at least from the beginning of the fourth century. What is unusual, however, is the direct invocation of Mary as intercessor at this early date. A few other texts, such as Gregory of Nyssa's panegyric on St Gregory the Wonderworker,[7] suggest that some Christians already believed in the Virgin's role as mediator in this period, but such references are scattered in comparison with accounts of other saints and their miracles.

One other interesting piece of evidence from the late fourth century is Epiphanius of Salamis's description of a "heretical" sect of women called the "Kollyridians." According his *Panarion* (a treatise written against many heresies, also entitled "The Medicine Chest"), compiled in about AD 374–77, the Kollyridians celebrated a service in honor of the Theotokos which involved the baking and offering of small loaves of bread ("kollyrides"). Epiphanius denounces this cult and states that while Christians

---

[6]See Shoemaker, "Marian Liturgies and Devotion in Early Christianity," in S.J. Boss, ed., *Mary: The Complete Resource* (London and New York: Continuum, 2007), 130. Shoemaker provides editions and other bibliography in his note 6.

[7]According to this text, Mary appeared to Gregory in a vision, accompanied by St John the Evangelist. She was shining in a blaze of light "as if a brilliant torch had been lit." If genuine, this testimony dates to the middle or second half of the third century, since Gregory the Wonderworker died in about 270. See PG 46, col. 912.

may honor the Theotokos, they should not worship her.[8] No other contemporary writers mention the Kollyridians, however, so it is difficult to verify the exact nature and popularity of this group.[9]

Moving into the fifth century, the evidence for Marian veneration in Constantinople begins to grow. The historian Sozomen, who was writing in the 440s, alludes to a healing cult at the church of Anastasia, which he associates with the Theotokos. He writes that a certain "dynamis" ("power") appears to people, either when they are awake or asleep, and cures them of their ailments, adding, "It is believed that this is Mary, Christ's mother, the holy Virgin, for she appears in that guise."[10] It is also in this period that the Virgin's most important relics, a robe and a belt, were transferred from Jerusalem and placed in churches in the imperial city. The literary evidence for these acquisitions is later, dating from the seventh century onward, but it is likely that both were installed, in the churches of Blachernae and Chalkoprateia respectively, by the end of the fifth century.[11] The miracles that were associated with these relics, recorded from about the seventh century onward, will be discussed below. For now, it is simply worth saying that although the evidence for the fifth century is scattered, it is clear that—in conjunction with the Christological discussions that were taking place in this period—veneration of the Mother

[8]Graef, *Mary: A History of Doctrine and Devotion*, 72–3.

[9]For a sceptical approach to the Kollyridian heresy, as described by Epiphanius, see Shoemaker, "Marian Liturgies," 132–4.

[10]Sozomen, *Ecclesiastical History*, Book VII. 5.1–4; cited and translated by C. Mango, "Constantinople as Theotokoupolis," in M. Vassilaki, ed., *Mother of God. Representations of the Virgin in Byzantine Art* (Milan and Athens: Skira, 2000), 17.

[11]Mango, "Constantinople as Theotokoupolis," 19.

of God, as intercessor and protector, was becoming an important aspect of Byzantine spirituality.

It is thus no accident that legends about the "falling asleep" (dormition), or death, of the Mother of God and her assumption into heaven, which may originally have circulated orally, began to be written down and disseminated from the late fifth century onward. Stephen Shoemaker has shown that various narratives existed in the Syriac and Greek Churches, with "families" of texts exhibiting distinct characteristics. One version, known as the "Palm of the Tree of Life" tradition, came to be accepted in Constantinopolitan circles. The earliest surviving texts that contain this version of the story include a sixth-century work known as the *Obsequies of the Holy Virgin* and a seventh-century homily by John of Thessalonica.

The story, as we saw in Chapter Three, concerns Mary's preparation for her own death (having been alerted to this event by an angel), the miraculous transportation of the twelve apostles to her bedside from their various missions around the inhabited world, and finally Christ's appearance in their midst. After the soul of the Theotokos has been released into his care, the apostles carry the body of the Theotokos to a tomb in Gethsemane. The story of the doubting Jew, Jephonias, occurs in this context, providing a cautionary teaching on the importance of faith in this mystery. After the deposition of the body, it rests in the tomb for three days before being assumed into heaven.

This narrative became the basis for the iconographical depiction of the scene that appears in later Byzantine icons: the Mother of God is shown at the moment of her death, with Christ receiving her soul (in the form of a swaddled baby) and the apostles clustered around the bed. Homilies, dating from the early seventh century onward, also commemorate the Dormition of the Virgin; as Antoine Wenger, Brian Daley, and other scholars have argued, Byzantine liturgical writers tend to treat this event with reverent caution. They make no attempt to explain in systematic terms the bodily assumption of the Mother of God into heaven. There is a tacit acceptance, however, in all of these liturgical texts, that the Virgin Mary was granted a destiny that is not open to other mortal beings apart from Christ. Furthermore, her ability to intercede on behalf of the rest of humanity from this exalted position could only have become more apparent as Christians reflected on the mystery. The Mother of God was pictured as a powerful and merciful presence at the heavenly throne; while remaining entirely human, she enjoyed divine favor in her glorious translation from this life to the next.

It was in the course of the sixth century that evidence for Mary's emerging role as protector and intercessor for Christians began to increase. The trend is first observable in Eastern Christendom, but it was soon followed in the West. The sixth-century Byzantine emperor Justinian encouraged the growing veneration of the Virgin: not only did he build a number of churches in her honor, but he began to establish feast-days commemorating her role in the Incarnation of Christ, beginning with the feast of the Annunciation (March 25). It is also possible, although not certain, that Justinian added the feast of Mary's Nativity, on September 8, to the calendar. Justinian's successors, Justin II and Maurice, were responsible for founding more churches and feasts in her honor, with the feast of the Dormition (August 15) being added to the calendar at the end of the sixth century.

In the early seventh century, another significant event occurred, which had a lasting impact on the cult of the Theotokos. The

Akathistos Hymn commemorates the miraculous lifting of the Persians' and Avars' siege of Constantinople in AD 626.[12] A number of historical sources describe the important role that the Virgin Mary played in this siege. If the Byzantines had succumbed on this occasion, the empire would have collapsed. According to three texts, including a homily by the Synkellos (or patriarchal assistant) Theodore, a chronicle, and a panegyrical poem, the Virgin Mary appeared on the walls of Constantinople at a critical moment of the final battle for the city, brandishing her sword and causing terror to the besieging armies.[13] Although these historical accounts vary slightly in their telling of the tale, they all refer to this miraculous event. It is probably as a result of this victory that a second prologue was added to the *Akathistos Hymn*, in which the Virgin Mary was celebrated for her protection of the capital city:

> To you, our leader in battle and defender,
> O Theotokos, I, your city, delivered from calamity,
> Offer hymns of victory and thanksgiving.
> Since you are invincible in power,
> Free me from every peril,
> That I may cry to you,
> "Hail, bride unwedded."[14]

[12]The hymn is translated in Mother Mary and Archimandrite Kallistos Ware, *The Lenten Triodion*, 422–37. For further discussion, see also above, Chapter Three, 82–4.

[13]For a full account, see B. Pentcheva, *Icons and Power. The Mother of God in Byzantium* (University Park, PA: Penn State University Press, 2006), 37–59.

[14]Trans. Mother Mary and Archimandrite Kallistos Ware, *The Lenten Triodion*, 422–23. This translation has been adjusted to follow the original text, which has the city, rather than the faithful, addressing the Theotokos.

Even before this victory had taken place, Mary was described in the same hymn, as we saw in Chapter Four, as the "unshaken fortress of the Church . . . unconquered rampart of the kingdom . . . through whom standards of victory are raised on high . . . [and] through whom enemies are cast down."[15]

What, meanwhile, was going on in the West between the fourth and seventh centuries? This was of course an eventful period, which saw the collapse of unified Roman rule and the emergence of smaller, usually Christian, kingdoms. There is not space here to discuss the many and complicated ramifications of these political events. The main development that is important for our purpose is that that the Latin and Greek-speaking halves of Christendom began to drift apart and to develop independent interpretations of Christian theology and tradition.

In spite of this tendency, it is possible to see parallel trends in the development of traditions surrounding the Virgin Mary in East and West. A number of Latin Fathers of the late fourth or early fifth centuries, including Ambrose, Augustine, and Jerome, wrote in her praise, emphasizing various aspects of her role in the Incarnation from a theological perspective. Themes of particular interest to these Fathers include Mary's virginity, both *in partu* and *post partum*, her unique relationship with Christ, and her personal piety. One such theme is the Latin Fathers' stress on Mary's role not only as mother of Christ, but also as mother of the Church. Augustine of Hippo writes on this subject, for example, as follows:

---

[15]Trans. Mother Mary and Archimandrite Kallistos Ware, *The Lenten Triodion*, 436 (with adjustments).

Therefore this woman alone, not only in spirit, but also in body, is both Mother and Virgin. She is Mother in the Spirit, but not of our Head, the Savior himself, for it is she who was spiritually born from him, since all who believe in him, among whom she too is to be counted, are rightly called children of the Bridegroom. Rather, she is clearly the Mother of his members; that is, of ourselves, because she cooperated by her charity, so that faithful Christians, members of the Head, might be born in the Church. As for the body, she is the Mother of his Head.[16]

Most early Latin Marian writings—and there are many—are thus theological in their emphasis; they explore the Virgin's relationship to Christ and humanity, stressing her importance in the divine dispensation of salvation.

The picture changes, however, by about the end of the sixth century, as we see in a few miracle stories that are transmitted by the bishop, Gregory of Tours. Interestingly enough, Gregory is also the first Western writer to bear witness to the Assumption of the Virgin into heaven, having received this legend from a fifth-century Latin translation of an apocryphal Greek text on the subject. Gregory was also responsible for collecting a number of stories in his "Book of Miracles," some of which relate to the Virgin Mary. Some of these concern holy places or objects that were associated with Mary in Palestine; others portray her as a powerful protector and intercessor.

---

[16] Augustine, *On Holy Virginity* 6; trans. L. Gambero, *Mary and the Fathers of the Church. The Blessed Virgin Mary in Patristic Thought* (San Francisco: Ignatius Press, 1999), 223.

Byzantine Devotion to the Virgin Mary

In the Byzantine empire, devotion to the Mother of God sometimes focused on the material objects through which divine power could be mediated. Miracles first came about through the Virgin's holy relics, the robe and belt, and somewhat later, probably from about the tenth century onward, through her icons.[17] We have already seen how, at the beginning of the seventh century, Mary was seen fighting on the walls of Constantinople by various witnesses in the course of the siege undertaken by the Avars and Persians. The account of another siege in 864, this time by the Rus' army, however, attributes Constantinople's deliverance directly to that the Virgin's robe, which was housed at the church of the Blachernae on the northern outskirts of the city. The patriarch Photius, in a sermon of thanksgiving delivered shortly after the end of the siege, describes the miraculous effect of a procession in which the holy relic was displayed to the enemy :

> For immediately as the Virgin's garment went around the walls, the barbarians gave up the siege, and broke camp, while we were delivered from impending capture and were granted unexpected salvation.[18]

Just under a century later, the emperor Romanus I Lecapenus (920–44) wrapped himself in the garment (which by now was being described as a "maphorion" or mantle) when he went to negotiate peace with the Bulgarian ruler Simeon in 926. Alexius I Comnenus used a piece of the relic as a standard on the battlefield

[17]Pentcheva, *Icons and Power,* 107, ff.

[18]Photius, *Homily* 4.4, trans. C. Mango, *The Homilies of Photius, Patriarch of Constantinople* (Cambridge, MA: Harvard University Press, 1958), 102–3.

in 1089, but hid it in a bush when the fighting became especially fierce![19] It is curious to note that after about 1204, the Virgin's robe and belt ceased to feature so often in Byzantine narratives concerning the capital city of Constantinople. At least one scholar argues that icons were beginning to replace relics in this period as foci of Marian veneration in the Byzantine Church.[20] Even as the holy garments of the Mother of God were dispersed in the later Byzantine centuries, however, they did not drop out of sight altogether. Her belt eventually came into the hands of Prince Lazar, ruler of Serbia, who bestowed it on the monastery of Vatopedi on Mount Athos, where it remains to this day.[21]

Hymnography

The liturgical texts of the Byzantine Church also reflect the growing prominence of the Mother of God—in both Christological and devotional terms—from about the fifth century onward. One of the most important genres, which has ancient roots but began to proliferate especially after the liturgical developments in the eighth and ninth centuries, was a short hymn, or troparion, known as a

[19]For an account of these events, and their importance the context of Marian relic veneration, see Pentcheva, *Icons and Power*, 63.

[20]Pentcheva, *Icons and Power*, 2.

[21]The relic has recently attracted media attention because it was taken to Russia in 2011, where many Orthodox Christians were able to venerate it. The belt is now described (although such details are absent in Byzantine sources) as having been made by the Mother of God herself out of strands of camel hair. She is said to have bestowed it on the disciple Thomas when he arrived late at her tomb and saw her ascending into heaven. It should be noted, however, that other churches also claim to possess this relic (or parts of it): these include the Roman Catholic cathedral in Prato, Tuscany, and the church of the Virgin's belt in Homs, Syria.

"theotokion." Theotokia could feature either at the end of each ode of the hymnographic form known as the kanon (which had its place in the monastic office of Matins) or on their own in various settings within the offices. Their assimilation into the kanon is particularly appropriate since the kanon teaches above all the fulfillment of the old covenant in the new. Mary, the Theotokos, represents the symbolic meeting place of the two Testaments: it is at the moment of her conception of the incarnate Christ that prophecy and typology are superseded by the reality of humanity's new relationship with God. A second, but related, form of hymn that developed in this period is the "stavrotheotokion" ("Cross-Theotokos hymn"), which explores the Virgin Mary's grief at the foot of the Cross; these are sung in the services of Wednesdays and Fridays, days that commemorate the passion of Christ and his cross. They replace the ordinary theotokia in the offices of most saints whose commemorations happen to fall on these days.

Of all the hymnographical forms, the theotokia are the most successful at combining Christological teaching with prayers to the Mother of God as intercessor. A few examples will suffice to illustrate this point. The first, which conveys a primarily Christological message but adds an invocation to the Theotokos in the final line, appears in Andrew of Crete's kanon on mid-Pentecost after the first ode:

> You alone, Birth-giver of God (Θεογεννῆτορ), contained the only Creator in your womb and you inexpressibly carried Him in the flesh and remained a Virgin, while your virginity was in no way despoiled. Beseech him, pure one, as your Son and God, always and without ceasing on behalf of your flock.[22]

[22]PG 97, 1421C.

In another kanon, this time on St Anna, by the same hymnographer, we see an invocation of Mary's intercessory power in the theotokion for Ode 4:

> Virgin, Theotokos, unblemished tabernacle, now purify me, who am defiled by my failings, with the most pure drops of your compassion, and give me a helping hand in order that I may cry, "Glory to you, pure one, who are glorified by God![23]

In addition to her special place in theotokia and stavrotheotokia, the Mother of God is celebrated throughout the hymnography of the offices and Divine Liturgy of the Byzantine—and modern—Orthodox Church. Hymns known as "kontakia," "dogmatika," "idiomela," "stichera," as well as the longer kanons, focus on Mary in relation to her blessed life, Christological importance, and intercessory role. Indeed, as we have seen throughout this book, the Mother of God represents a primary focus in Orthodox reflection on the meaning of the Incarnation: she is the place where the divine and created realms meet and where Christians first encounter the incarnate Son. Mary also represents humanity in kneeling at the foot of the cross in grief and bearing witness to his Resurrection and Ascension into heaven.

"Popular" Texts on the Intercession of the Theotokos

Before concluding this chapter, it is important to mention one other group of Byzantine texts that helped to influence Orthodox Christian devotion to the Mother of God. This consists of what we might call "popular" forms of literature, including miracle

[23]PG 97, 1309b.

stories and more apocalyptic texts. To begin with the miracle stories, these short texts are often associated with a particular church or shrine in honor of the Mary the Theotokos. One such collection is that associated with a holy spring ("pegē") just outside the walls of Constantinople. The tales, which were collected over a number of centuries, relate healings and other miracles that took place at the spring. They celebrate the faith of those who visited the shrine, as well as the power of the Mother of God that could be accessed through the holy water.[24]

Another interesting literary genre, which grew in popularity after the end of Iconoclasm in AD 843, is that of the "apocalypse." This form of narrative, which is concerned especially with the fate of Christians after death, originated in the early Christian period but continued to circulate in the medieval period and beyond. Originally written in Greek, these texts were translated into Latin, Slavonic, and many other languages. They survive in numerous manuscripts, a fact that testifies to their popularity among Christians throughout the centuries. The modern editor of the probably ninth-century *Apocalypse of the Holy Theotokos*, M.R. James, describes it as "monotonous, quite contemptible as literature, and even positively repulsive in places."[25] This judgment, which is echoed by Ivan in *The Brothers Karamazov*,[26] is perhaps a

---

[24]Alice-Mary Talbot and Scott Fitzgerald Johnson, trans., *Miracle Tales from Byzantium,* Dumbarton Oaks Medieval Library 12 (Washington, DC: Dumbarton Oaks, 2012).

[25]M.R. James, *Apocrypha Anecdota*, Texts and Studies 2.3 (Cambridge: Cambridge University Press, 1893), 110.

[26]Fyodor Dostoyevsky, *The Brothers Karamazov*, trans. D. McDuff (London: Penguin Books, 1980; rev. ed. 2003), 322–23 (at the beginning of Chapter Five: "The Grand Inquisitor").

reaction to the simplistic—and not altogether appealing—view of divine retribution that is conveyed in this apocalyptic text. Jane Baun has pointed to its importance as a window into medieval spirituality, arguing that it can tell us much about ordinary Christians' understanding of Mary's role as intercessor.[27]

The *Apocalypse of the Holy Theotokos* describes, like many other texts of this type, a visionary experience of the afterlife. Mary, the "Panagia" ("all-holy one"), while praying on the Mount of Olives, asks for information about the punishments that human beings experience after death and about the nature of heaven and hell. In response to this prayer, the archangel Michael, accompanied by many other angels, appears to her and acclaims her holiness and power as Mother of God. Michael then takes her on a tour of Hades, or hell, where Mary sees various categories of sinners being punished with tortures that are appropriate to their misdeeds. The Mother of God asks to be taken into the presence of God the Father himself. On arriving at the foot of his throne, she begs him to forgive the sinners whose plight she has just witnessed, in the following words:

> Have mercy, O Master, on the Christian sinners; for I have seen them being punished and I cannot bear their lamentation. May I go forth, and may I myself be punished with the Christian sinners![28]

When God responds sternly to this prayer, the Mother of God calls on the whole angelic host to join her in supplication. Both

[27]Jane Baun, *Tales From Another Byzantium. Celestial Journey and Local Community in the Medieval Greek Apocrypha* (Cambridge: Cambridge University Press, 2007).

[28]Baun, *Tales From Another Byzantium*, 398.

Father and Son eventually relent, but they only allow the sinners in Hades to enjoy a brief respite from their sufferings between Pascha and Pentecost.

We are led to ask, in response to texts such as this, how they fit in with more conventional expressions of the Virgin Mary's role as intercessor in the Byzantine Orthodox tradition. As we have already seen, many liturgical texts, including homilies, hymns, and prayers, call on the Mother of God as Christians' main intermediary before God. Such invocations always stress her importance in Christological doctrine, as Virgin and God-bearer, as well as her obedience and humility as the "Second Eve." The Virgin Mary has freedom of speech ("παρρησία") both because of her privileged position as Christ's mother and as a result of her Assumption into heaven after death.

The difference, according to each of these ways of portraying the Virgin Mary's intercessory role in Byzantine tradition, is above all one of emphasis. Whereas apocalypses, such as the ninth-century example that is described above, portray Mary's relationship with God as involving some tension, liturgical texts (including both homilies and hymns) suggest an ordered, reciprocal arrangement in which the Mother of God appeals to a merciful Savior. According to mainstream liturgical tradition, the Theotokos works within seamlessly united heavenly and earthly spheres, through which God's power flows with the help of her mediation.

The question whether texts such as apocalypses reveal a heterodox tendency in Byzantine culture may never be solved in a satisfactory way.[29] What is important, in relation to such texts, is

[29]Jane Baun calls this tradition "paracanonical" in order to express its deviation from "official" Orthodox narratives surrounding the Mother of God.

that we understand their literary contexts, audiences or readers, and dissemination in medieval society. It is likely that such colorful descriptions of heaven and hell were written as much for entertainment as to convey moral teaching. Perhaps Byzantine Christians, when reading or listening to such narratives, would have known how to place them within a wider understanding, gained mostly from liturgical texts, of the Virgin Mary's Christological stature.

Scholars have recently been searching for evidence that might tell us more about popular spirituality, employing not only literary witnesses but also a variety of media including seals, amulets, embroidered clothing, icons, and other objects.[30] Such sources bear witness to widespread Marian devotion in the medieval Byzantine period (that is, approximately between the seventh and fifteenth centuries) but, owing to the scattered nature of such evidence, it is often difficult to determine their provenance. Questions such as whether women, the less educated, or other groups within this society were particularly devoted to the Mother of God are difficult, if not impossible, to answer. In any case, it is clear that Byzantine Christians had access to a rich and varied tradition surrounding Mary, the Mother of God. This was expressed, as we have seen, by means of literary and liturgical texts, relics, icons, feasts, and many other media—some of which may have

See her article, "Discussing Mary's humanity in medieval Byzantium," in R.N. Swanson, ed., *The Church and Mary, Studies in Church History* 39 (Woodbridge: Boydell and Brewster, 2004), 63–72.

[30]See, for example, Baun, "Discussing Mary's humanity", 71–72; B. Pitarakis, "Female piety in context: understanding developments in private devotional contexts," in M. Vassilaki, ed., *Images of the Mother of God. Perceptions of the Theotokos in Byzantium* (Aldershot: Ashgate, 2005), 153–66.

been transmitted orally or otherwise lost, owing to the historical events that separate this Christian empire from modern Orthodox communities.

Veneration of the Mother of God, as Intercessor, in the Orthodox Church Today

So far our discussion has focused on early Christian and medieval ideas about Mary's intercessory role in the Church. How do modern Orthodox Christians view the Mother of God and how do they venerate her, in both Christological and devotional terms? These questions can be answered in various ways—just as they could be in the past—since Christians relate to the Mother of God on so many levels.

First, it is necessary to emphasize the centrality of Mary's place in the mystery of the Incarnation that is so deeply embedded in Orthodox Christians' liturgical and devotional experience. The hymns and icons that adorn each Orthodox feast-day reinforce the sense that Mary represents a meeting-place for the divine and created states of being. God entered the world as the Incarnate Son with the assent and cooperation of this young girl; he also took his human flesh, or physical nature, from her alone. Mary thus plays her role in this mystery in both metaphysical and ethical terms: she provides Christ with his human nature and also freely accepts her role in this mystery.

When Orthodox Christians pray to the Mother of God in the context of liturgical worship or in private, they are guided by tradition to use words that consistently recall the Christological basis for such veneration. As we have seen in the course of this chapter, most prayers or hymns, such as the short theotokia that are attached to each stanza of the kanons that are sung in Matins, allude to Mary's role in the Incarnation even as they allow the Christian to pray for her intercession and help. Sometimes liturgical texts may seem to blur the boundary between Mary as *source* of protection or as its *mediator*; in strict theological terms, of course, such assistance can only come from God himself. An idiomelon in the fourth tone, sung at Vespers on August 15 (the feast of the Dormition), could cause confusion:

> Praising her as Mother of God, we cry and say, "From all distress save us who confess you, O Theotokos, and grant our souls deliverance from tribulation."[31]

While passages such as this—as well as the repeated prayer "Most Holy Theotokos, save us!"—may appear to attribute all help and protection to the Mother of God, they should not read in isolation. Most liturgical texts emphasize, as we have seen, the Christological role that enables Mary to act as intercessor between God and humanity. In almost every case, she does not take the Son's place as the main Christian mediator; rather, she represents, like angels and saints, an approachable figure in the heavenly sphere, who enables faithful worshippers to draw closer to their Savior.

The Orthodox Christian tradition has consistently emphasized Mary's humanity. Liturgical and doctrinal texts stress the fact that she was conceived in a normal way (even if, according to tradition, this conception was miraculously granted to Joachim and Anna who had previously been sterile) and that she actually died before being assumed into heaven. It is perhaps in order

---

[31]Mother Mary and Archimandrite Kallistos Ware, trans., *The Festal Menaion*, 510–11 (with adjustments).

to reinforce this truly human aspect of the Mother of God that icons portray her in simple, dark garments that are unadorned by decoration or jewelry. Many, especially later, icons also draw attention to Mary's emotional state, which is usually one of tenderness and sadness as if she is contemplating the inevitable death of her beloved Son. Such a portrayal of the Mother of God, which reflects a Christology that was carefully worked out in the course of the first five centuries, lends itself to a form of devotion that is mindful of Mary's proximity to the human condition of the Christian faithful.

Thus, Orthodox Christians pray to the Mother of God for intercession and help in many situations. In accepting from a very early date, as we have seen, the special access that the Virgin Mary provides to her Son—whether as his mother or as one who now sits beside him in heaven—Orthodox tradition has endorsed devotion to this holy figure. For the most part, liturgical texts, narratives, and icons stress Mary's humanity even while depicting her purity, freedom from sin, and dignity. Some texts, such as the medieval apocalypses that were mentioned above, may stray into more fanciful exploration of tension between the Virgin's merciful intentions and God's righteous judgment; even in these, however, a sense of orderly hierarchy is maintained. We may question the need for another mediator besides the Savior, Jesus Christ, but liturgical texts again provide the answer. Mary, according to the Fathers who produced the hymns and prayers that continue to be used today, is inevitably involved in human salvation because of her role in bringing Christ, as incarnate Lord, into the world. As the ninth-century hymnographer, Joseph, puts it:

You wove for the world a crown not made with human hands, and we sing your praises, as we cry aloud, "Hail to you, Virgin, the guardian of all, fortress and stronghold and sacred refuge!"[32]

Further Reading:

Boss, Sarah Jane. *Mary: The Complete Resource*, Part II: "The Cult of the Virgin Mary During the Middle Ages." London & New York: Continuum, 2007, 147–203.

Boulet, Juliet du. *Portrait of a Greek Mountain Village*. Oxford: Clarendon Press, 1974.

Cameron, Averil. "The Theotokos in Sixth-century Constantinople. A City Finds its Symbol." *Journal of Theological Studies*, n.s. 29 (1978), 79–108.

Cameron, Averil. "The Virgin's Robe: An Episode in the History of Early Seventh-century Constantinople." *Byzantion* 49 (1979), 42–56.

Peltomaa, Leena Mari. *The Image of the Virgin Mary in the Akathistos Hymn*. Leiden, Boston, and Cologne: Brill, 2001.

Pentcheva, Bissera. *Icons and Power. The Mother of God in Byzantium*. University Park, PA: Penn State University Press, 2006.

Talbot, Alice-Mary and Johnson, Scott Fitzgerald, trans., *Miracle Tales from Byzantium*, Dumbarton Oaks Medieval Library 12 (Washington, DC: Dumbarton Oaks, 2012).

[32]Joseph the Hymnographer, Kanon of the Akathistos, Ode 4; trans. Archimandrite Ephrem at <http://www.anastasis.org.uk/akathist.htm>.

chapter seven

MODERN ORTHODOX INTERPRETATIONS OF THE MOTHER OF GOD: SYMBOL OF WISDOM AND MODEL FOR HUMANKIND

Reflection on Mary, the Mother of God, in the modern period (that is, from about the end of the nineteenth century onward) has flourished in both oral and written contexts. Sermons continue to be delivered on the great Marian feasts, while theological publications expound the Virgin's role in the Incarnation and in the Church. In this chapter we will explore some of the insights about Mary that have emerged in the last hundred years or so, focusing on a few of the themes that modern theologians have emphasized in relation to this diverse and rich topic.

It is impossible to be comprehensive in our coverage of modern approaches to Mary in a book of this size. For this reason, I have chosen to focus on several schools of thought or individual theologians who have contributed profound ideas relating to the Mother of God. We will begin with the Russian "Sophiological" school of

theology associated mostly with Sergei Bulgakov, with its emphasis on Mary's role as the creaturely embodiment of "Wisdom"
or "Sophia." Such interest in the way in which God manifests
himself throughout creation, and especially in the Spirit-bearing
figure of the Mother of God, is also found in the thought of the
English theologian, Philip Sherrard. Another twentieth-century
Orthodox theologian, Vladimir Lossky, has offered a vision of the
Mother of God as a faithful follower and disciple of Christ. Several contemporary Orthodox thinkers, including Elisabeth Behr-
Sigel and Wendy Robinson, have also emphasized Mary's place
as model for humanity. This preoccupation reveals an awareness
of her presence in the hearts and minds of all Orthodox Christians, as the human being who—before all others—opened herself
to God and freely chose to accept his will. Other contemporary
theologians, including John Behr and Metropolitan Kallistos of
Diokleia, have looked at further aspects of Mary's character and
way of life. These include, respectively, her role as symbol of the
Church and her silence, as one who "kept all these things and
pondered them in her heart" (Lk 2.19).

Modern perceptions of Mary's role in Orthodox Christian tradition are usually framed in a devotional, rather than systematic,
form of discourse. This approach, which consciously distances
itself from the dogmatic or historical approaches that often char-
acterize Marian Studies in the West, preserves the mystery that
has traditionally surrounded the Mother of God in Orthodox
thought. As we shall see in Chapter Eight, however, there are
areas in which the Christian East and West overlap and offer
mutual benefit. It is my intention to describe here a few strands
of modern Orthodox reflection on the Virgin Mary that are particularly meaningful and interesting—even if some of these, such

as the idea of her role as "Sophia," failed to gain acceptance in the long term.

Mary as symbol of "Wisdom"

Sergei Bulgakov (1871–1944) devoted considerable space in his writings to Mary, the Mother of God. Two main works, *The Burning Bush* and *The Bride of the Lamb*, place her at the center of God's ongoing involvement with his own creation. Although Bulgakov's work is currently experiencing a revival, with scholarly recognition of his bold and exploratory approach to theology, it is seen to stray in certain ways from mainstream Orthodox tradition.[1] Building on the Russian philosophical movement that embraced a Platonic understanding of the Biblical image of Wisdom, as revealed in Old Testament books such as Proverbs and Ecclesiastes, Bulgakov presents Mary as the archetypal example of this divine figure in creation. This is not to say that the Virgin *is* Wisdom; rather, she represents in her person the "sophianic" image that God intended for all human beings. This is the way in which divine attributes may be manifested in creation, when a holy and entirely pure person such as Mary becomes a "bearer of the Holy Spirit."

For Bulgakov, the Virgin Mary offers an image of humanity— indeed of all creation—as God intended it to be. As a created being who shares in the fallen state of Adam and Eve, Mary is subject to death and the tendency to sin that afflicts the rest of humanity. Bulgakov saw the Fall, in both literal and symbolic terms, as a cosmic catastrophe. It disrupted the harmonious state, mediated

---

[1]See, for example, the essays assembled in *St Vladimir's Theological Quarterly* 49, nos. 1–2 (2005).

by the figure of Wisdom, which should exist in the universe as God planned it. The Mother of God helped to restore creation to its intended role as receptacle and mirror of divine being in two ways: she accepted God's incarnation as Christ in her womb at the Annunciation, but she also became a "Spirit-bearing" person in herself, as one who manifested God's Wisdom in this world.

Bulgakov's theology may sometimes be worded in an unusual way, but it is largely faithful to Orthodox tradition concerning the Mother of God. As we see especially in the more systematic and occasionally polemical treatise, *The Burning Bush*, Bulgakov is keen to emphasize Mary's full humanity, and sees the Roman Catholic dogma of the Immaculate Conception as seriously jeopardizing it. Thus Bulgakov emphasizes Mary's actual death before she was assumed into heaven (also undermined in some Roman Catholic popular teaching), as well as the idea that she developed gradually into a fully sanctified state. The Annunciation and Pentecost represented important stages in this process: on each occasion, Mary was blessed by the grace of the Holy Spirit. Bulgakov writes:

> . . . the most holy Virgin is not a personal incarnation of the Holy Spirit, but she becomes his personal, animate receptacle, an absolutely spirit-born creature, the Pneumatophoric Human . . . In this complete penetration by [the Holy Spirit] it becomes a different nature for its own self, i.e. divinized, a creature thoroughly blessed by grace, "a quickened ark of God," a living, "consecrated temple."[2]

[2]S. Bulgakov, *The Burning Bush. On the Orthodox Veneration of the Mother of God*, trans. T.A. Smith (Grand Rapids, MI and Cambridge: William Eerdmans Publishing Co., 2009), 81.

The Mother of God thus represents for Bulgakov the intersection between divine and created being. Not only did she enable God to become incarnate, by giving him her physical nature, but she manifested divinity, in its "sophianic" form, in the created world. Mary is the quintessential example, in other words, of *theosis*, or deification, in the human race. Whereas Christ, as God-man, uniquely combined divine and human natures in one person, Mary, as a fully human person, assumed the divine image and likeness that had been intended for all mankind. Bulgakov also adopts Russian sophiological ideas concerning the God-given characteristics of masculine and feminine gender: whereas Christ, the Logos, represents the former, Sophia, or Wisdom—who is mediated by the Holy Spirit—provides a feminine dimension in the ongoing relationship between God and his creation.

It is difficult to summarize here the complexity of Bulgakov's thought, which seeks to maintain an Orthodox Christological perspective while explaining how God manifests himself, in both Christ and Mary, in the Church. He draws not only on the conciliar tradition, especially as expressed at Chalcedon in 451, but also on the rich Biblical and liturgical understanding of God's immanence in creation through his Incarnation. While acknowledging that there is neither male nor female in Christ (Gal 3.28), Bulgakov sees his embodiment in the Church as being manifested in what he calls a "bi-unitary hypostasis": Christ became "incarnate by the Holy Spirit, Jesus-Mary, the all-human being and the divine human being, the uncreated Proto-image of the human being and the created image of God."[3] Such language will perhaps sound unfamiliar to Orthodox Christians, but if we

[3]S. Bulgakov, *The Bride of the Lamb*, trans. B. Jakim (Edinburgh: T. & T. Clark, 2002), 99.

try to penetrate to the meaning that Bulgakov seeks to convey it becomes more understandable. He is placing Mary at the center of the Incarnation, in keeping with Patristic tradition, insisting that the unity—in ontological terms—between Christ and his Mother is reflected in the Church:

> This dual-unity is preserved in unity. The male nature is hypostasized in Christ in his relation to the Church, as the head of the body of Christ, while the female nature is hypostasized in relation to him as the Bridegroom of the Church: "Thee, my Wife, I love."[4]

Mary, according to this vision, becomes in an important sense a symbol of this cosmic marriage:

> And in this love for Christ, the character of the love of the Lord's Servant, the Mother of God, is revealed. This character consists in the fact that she "humbles" herself both empirically and ontologically, stops being for herself, becomes transparent for the hypostasis of her Son, reveals this hypostasis, as is proper to the third hypostasis, the Holy Spirit, in the supra-eternal love in the Holy Trinity . . .[5]

While Bulgakov's thought may at first strike Orthodox readers as strange, even Gnostic in its emphasis on Sophia who seems to appear as a fourth, feminine figure within the Godhead, his writings merit careful study. It is partly in opposition to the complete

---

[4]Bulgakov, *The Bride of the Lamb*, 100. This passage must allude to the Book of Revelation, which contrasts the wanton harlot and the faithful bride as images of God's broken covenant with Israel and his new one, as Bridegroom, with the Church.

[5]Bulgakov, *The Bride of the Lamb*, 99.

separation between God and creation that he perceived in Western theology that Bulgakov developed his ideas about divinity manifesting itself both through the Incarnation of Christ and through the "sophianic" witness of the Mother of God. While acknowledging the unity of all things in the incarnate Christ, Bulgakov wanted to preserve the diversity, and above all the feminine and masculine aspects of God's creation, within this body. Mary stands at the center of this conjunction, representing both humanized divinity (since God was present in her womb) and divinized humanity.

Paul Evdokimov (1902–1970) was, like Sergei Bulgakov, a Russian émigré who spent most of his adult life in Paris, teaching at the Theological Institute of St Sergius. Also like Bulgakov, Evdokimov was an enthusiastic adherent of the Sophiological philosophical school. Statements that he makes about Mary, the Mother of God, may recall Bulgakov, as we see in the following passage taken from Evdokimov's major work, *Woman and the Salvation of the World*:

> [Mary] is the figure of the Wisdom of God. Through her, feminine spirituality is sophianic, intimately linked to the Holy Spirit.[6]

Even more than Bulgakov, however, Evdokimov is interested in exploring the place of women in God's creation. He believes, like other Sophiologists, in the existence of both masculine and feminine aspects of the divine nature: the feminine is hypostasized especially in the Holy Spirit and in that mediating principle

[6]P. Evdokimov, *Woman and the Salvation of the World. A Christian Anthropology on the Charisms of Women*, trans. A.P. Gythiel (Crestwood, NY: St Vladimir's Seminary Press, 1994), 153.

between God and his creation, Wisdom. Evdokimov associates certain qualities with these masculine and feminine principles: whereas the male attributes include power, adventurousness, and creativity, the female ones comprise receptivity, sensitivity, and the desire to nurture. Evdokimov argues that it is the latter that is most conducive to spirituality. He associates atheism with extreme masculinity, but religiosity with more feminine characteristics.[7] It is for this reason, he writes slightly later, that it was the Virgin Mary who received the message of salvation at the Annunciation:

> The one who gives birth to the Eternal God, the one who gives human life to the Ever-Living One, is herself immortalized. It is in this magnificent sense that Eve is called *Life* (Gen3.20). Now we can understand why it is the woman who received the message of salvation. The message of the Annunciation is addressed to a woman; the risen Christ appears first to a woman, and it is "the woman robed with the sun" (Rev12.1) who represents the New Jerusalem. *Scripture exalts woman as the religious element of human nature.* Woman is the mouth of humanity through which the humble "Be it unto me" (*fiat*) of the servant of God replied to the creative *fiat* ("Let it be done") of the heavenly Father. Woman is this free "Amen" of all of humanity which, in the work of the Incarnation, becomes the indispensable human foundation.[8]

Such statements should not be read literally—indeed, Evdokimov did not intend this to be interpreted as a demarcation of separate

---

[7]Evdokimov, *Woman and the Salvation of the World*, 152.

[8]Evdokimov, *Woman and the Salvation of the World*, 156.

roles for men and women in the Church. He meant, as Bulgakov did too, that the Church as a whole offers a feminine response, as Bride of Christ, to God the Father. Mary, who led the way in responding to this call, stands for the Church. The two halves of creation, male and female, are thereby united in a loving relationship; this cosmic union is reflected within each human person when both feminine and masculine qualities are acknowledged and the life in Christ is fully experienced.

Although Paul Evdokimov's promotion of women, along with what he regarded as feminine attributes, is advanced when set against some more traditional ideas in Orthodox thought, it did not ally itself with the secular feminism of his day. He rejected the stance of thinkers such as Simone de Beauvoir, which he saw ultimately as de-feminizing and nihilist in its aims.[9] He did explore, with enthusiasm, the ever-intriguing field of ancient mythology with its female goddesses and matriarchal leaders. However, when Evdokimov returned to the place of the Theotokos within Orthodox Christian tradition, he recognized the unique and mysterious nature of her relationship with God. He wrote that "the entire meaning of Mariological dogma is contained in the event of the birth of God."[10] Mary represents the place where divine and created natures came together, while also being the human being who freely turned towards God and gave him her assent. These are feminine qualities, but they are shared by the whole human race, which is involved in these acts of fecundity and assent.

[9]Evdokimov, *Woman and the Salvation of the World*, 183–84.

[10]Evdokimov, *Woman and the Salvation of the World*, 211. We should note here, as always in Orthodox Christian tradition, that "birth" here refers to the whole process of birth-giving, from conception to delivery of the baby.

The connection with creation

We have seen, in passing, Paul Evdokimov's focus on the Virgin Mary's role as fertile ground in which God was planted. This image has its origin in the typological connection between the untilled ground of paradise, from which God made Adam, and Mary's virginal body in which Christ, the second Adam, was conceived. Evdokimov underlines the earthy meaning of the image, which evokes Mary's physical connection with the rest of creation, in a passage in which he quotes an old woman's prophecy in Dostoyevsky's *The Possessed*:

> The Mother of God is the Great Mother—the damp earth (Gen 2.6); and therein lies a great joy for men.[11]

Another Orthodox theologian who has recently emphasized the importance of the Virgin Mary's links with material creation, according to liturgical tradition, is Philip Sherrard. In one of his books, which defends the holistic vision of Orthodox theology, Sherrard describes the Mother of God as

> . . . a passive potency, the "immaterial matter" in whom the Image-archetypes "take flesh," or "take body," though not initially a material, physical body. She is the universal spiritual substance, the universal Nature—*Natura naturans*—in which flower all the forms of being—everything that is differentiated from God's being as such—from the highest archangels down to the most elementary material organisms.[12]

[11]Evdokimov, *Woman and the Salvation of the World*, 153, quoting F. Dostoyevsky, *The Possessed*, ch. 4.

[12]P. Sherrard, *Human Image: World Image. The Death and Resurrection of Sacred Cosmology* (Ipswich: Golgonooza Press, 1992), 177.

Such language has overtones of the Sophiological school of thought that we have just been examining; Sherrard places Mary at the center of a cosmic vision of divine and human interaction. He also posits a "divine feminine principle," which he names as Sophia or Holy Wisdom, which is both "situated in God and other than God." Sherrard is careful, however, to differentiate God and his feminine counterpart, Wisdom: "they are linked together in their very being" but they do not share an essential nature. The relationship, which is hierarchical, is eternally expressed in both unity and "otherness."[13]

Where does Mary, the Mother of God, fit into this vision? According to Sherrard, she fulfils both a cosmic and a personal role in the dispensation. He associates her with the universal sphere of existence in which she gives birth to "Image-archetypes" that are in turn manifested in the visible world. However, in a personal sense, Mary gave birth to the God-man, Christ, at a particular moment in historical time. This represented the culmination of God's plan for creation, when he would himself enter and transfigure it with divine being. The Virgin Mary is thus the physical *locus* or receptacle in which this mystery takes place:

> The theandric mystery—the mystery of God-manhood, of the Incarnate Logos—is, then, that through which the sacramental reality of the created world is consummated. And the being through whom it is consummated is the Mother of God, whether in her universal plenitude as divine Wisdom or as the individualization of this Wisdom in the person of the all-holy Virgin Mary . . . Thus the Mother of God is not simply the foundation of the world of creatures: she is herself

[13]Sherrard, *Human Image: World Image*, 178.

this world. While remaining always spiritual, above space and time, she is also the root of what is material, spatial and temporal . . . She is Earth as a single immaterial feminine divinity, and she is earth as a manifold, material reality. She is herself the Body of the cosmic Christ, the created matrix in whom the divine Logos eternally takes flesh. She is the bridge that unites God to the world, the world to God, and it is she that bestows on the world its eternal and sacred value. She is the seal of its sacred identity.[14]

Mary as model for humanity

Such high-flown, philosophical ideas about the Mother of God may not strike a chord with every reader, even those that are accustomed to the praise that is normally offered to her in Orthodox liturgical services. Where, we might ask, is Mary, the humble Jewish girl from Nazareth? Are we in danger of forgetting the New Testament witness, which emphasizes her normal—and even at times doubting or grieving—human qualities? Some Orthodox theologians have recently focused on Mary's humanity, reminding us that she is a figure whom we can admire and emulate. It is indeed her human qualities that make the Virgin Mary accessible to us, as mother and intercessor.

Let us begin with Vladimir Lossky, who wrote a short but significant article entitled "Panagia" in 1950.[15] In relation to the

[14]Sherrard, *Human Image: World Image*, 181.

[15]First published in the journal, *Le Messager* 4 (1950), 40–50, this article is reprinted in V. Lossky, *In the Image and Likeness of God*, ed. J.H. Erickson and T.E. Bird (Crestwood, NY: St Vladimir's Seminary Press, 2001), 195–210.

passage in Luke that is sometimes seen as problematic, as regards the Church's veneration of the Mother of God, in which Christ appears to oppose her glorification by responding, "Blessed rather are those who hear the Word of God and keep it," to a woman who cries out, "Blessed is the womb that bore you, and the breasts that you sucked," (Lk 11. 27–28), Lossky reminds us that it is this very passage that is read solemnly in the great Marian feasts. The passage reminds us of the Virgin Mary's discipleship, which stands as an example to all of Christ's other disciples and to all Christians.[16] Lossky also sees the Mother of God as a testament to the importance of tradition, as well as Scripture, in the formation of Christian doctrine. Whereas the Old and New Testaments are relatively silent about her life, the events of which are celebrated in her feasts, apocryphal and liturgical texts have filled in these gaps—all being validated in the active life of the Church. For Lossky, the Virgin Mary is above all pure and open to accepting the Incarnation of the Word. She is, in short, the highest example of a deified human being. She realized her fullness and became manifest in the Church, to be glorified by all generations (Lk 1.48).[17]

Elisabeth Behr-Sigel devoted a chapter to the Mother of God in her influential book, *The Ministry of Women in the Church*.[18] Although the French theologian covers many aspects of Orthodox liturgical and theological reflection on the Mother of God, a theme that runs through her discussion is that of Mary's humanity.

---

[16]Lossky, *In the Image and Likeness of God*, 197.

[17]Lossky, *In the Image and Likeness of God*, 201.

[18]E. Behr-Sigel, *The Ministry of Women in the Church*, trans. S. Bigham (Redondo Beach, CA: Oakwood Publications, 1991), 181–216.

In this context, it is the young girl's acceptance of God's will at the scene of the Annunciation that is most significant. Behr-Sigel stresses the fact that Mary freely chose to accept the archangel's message in this passage:

> Mary conceived by an act of her free will and *became mother by a free choice. She was thus not just a simple passive instrument in the hands of an artist, but she rather offered herself and became co-worker with* God for the providence of mankind, thus associated with the glory that was to be the result.[19]

Behr-Sigel reveals similar preoccupations here to those that were often expressed by Metropolitan Anthony (Bloom) of Sourozh when he preached in the Russian cathedral in London on the Mother of God. Quoting the novelist Charles Williams, he writes as follows about the Annunciation:

> [Williams] says that when the time was right, a maiden of Israel proved capable of pronouncing the name of God with all her mind and all her will and all her flesh, and the Word became flesh. It is a gift of self, and it is at the same time an unreserved and heroic acceptance: a gift of self in humility, and an heroic acceptance because of what it could have been, what is meant humanly speaking.[20]

Both Behr-Sigel and Metropolitan Anthony present the Virgin Mary as someone who stands for all of us: she is entirely human

[19]Behr-Sigel, *The Ministry of Women in the Church*, 195 (italics are the author's).

[20]Metropolitan Anthony of Sourozh, "The Mother of God," *Sourozh* 21 (1980), 22–33.

and is faced with a momentous decision. That she chose to obey God affects us all since it brought glorious consequences and the hope of eternal life. However, we should not forget that such decisions continue to face us every day; we must hope and pray that, like the Mother of God, we will choose the right path, opening our hearts to God in full obedience and humility.

Interestingly, especially in comparison with the Sophiological ideas that we have just explored, Behr-Sigel also examines Mary's female nature and its meaning for the Church. Like her Russian colleagues, Behr-Sigel evokes the Virgin's symbolic role as the feminine spiritual principle that "has its foundation in the very life of the Trinity itself." After praising the work of Bulgakov and Evdokimov, however, she warns that turning masculine and feminine principles into existential realities risks obscuring "the basic category of *person* as the image of God in man (*anthropos*)."[21] This leads her to the conclusion that in spite of Mary's feminine gender, she stands in Orthodox tradition as a model for *all* human beings, male and female. This observation is supported by historical research, as we saw in Chapter Six, which suggests that the Virgin has been venerated throughout history equally by women and men.[22] While Behr-Sigel, like Evdokimov, relates the qualities of openness and sensitivity especially with women, she argues that all human beings possess these attributes. Men are sometimes slower to discover this receptivity within themselves and, as Behr-Sigel suggests, may find it with the help of a woman in their lives, such as a mother, wife, sister, or friend. Nevertheless, "the femininity of the Mother of God shows us the basic structure

[21]Behr-Sigel, *The Ministry of Women in the Church*, 208–9.

[22]See above, Chapter Six, pp. 148–9.

of humanity at its highest vocation, the call to holiness."[23] This conclusion does not significantly affect Behr-Sigel's call to Orthodox Christians to reconsider the vocations that are open to men and women, but it does serve to heighten our awareness of the dignity of women and their importance in the Church.

Wendy Robinson, the late and distinguished Orthodox psychotherapist who was a frequent speaker at Christian gatherings in the United Kingdom in recent years, also stresses Mary's humanity in a recent article.[24] She reminds us of the continual presence of the Mother of God in our lives and in the Church, citing the constant invocation of this holy figure in hymns and litanies. She is a figure of tenderness, love, and compassion, ever present to the Orthodox faithful who call on her. But beyond this, Robinson points to the silence, or mystery, that lies at the heart of Orthodox veneration of the Mother of God. Yet there is paradox here too:

> There is a certain silence around her mysteries. Yet this numinous, awe-inspiring and luminous, light-giving silence has always been endlessly inspirational. One moment we have teaching on the apophatic need to move beyond images, to honour silence and venerate the mysteries. The next moment we have mysteries breaking forth as if from a breathtaking treasure-house.[25]

[23]Behr-Sigel, *The Ministry of Women in the Church*, 212.

[24]W. Robinson, "Mary: The Flower and Fruit of Worship: The Mother of God in the Orthodox Tradition", in J. Behr, A. Louth, and D. Conomos, eds., *Abba: The Tradition of Orthodoxy in the West. Festschrift for Bishop Kallistos (Ware) of Diokleia* (Crestwood, NY: St Vladimir's Seminary Press, 2003), 193–205.

[25]Robinson, "Mary: The Flower and Fruit of Worship," 195.

Mary as Silence

This brings us to a theme that is also pursued by Metropolitan Kallistos of Diokleia in an article published in the proceedings of an ecumenical conference on the Virgin Mary.[26] Inspired by a homily written by Gregory Palamas for the feast of the Entry of the Mother of God into the temple (November 21),[27] Metropolitan Kallistos reminds us of the Biblical allusions to Mary's silence. "Hesychia, stillness or silence of the heart, is basically nothing else than an attitude of attentive listening."[28] The Virgin Mary, in her silence, listened to the word of God at the Annunciation, at the marriage feast in Cana, and on many other occasions as she followed and supported Christ in his ministry. Beyond this, however, the apocryphal *Protevangelium of James* describes her formation as a child in the temple. Having cut off her ties with all earthly things on entering the temple, Mary lived for nine years in the archetypal place of stillness: the holy of holies, communing only with God and his angels. Gregory Palamas builds on this theme in his homily, suggesting that the Virgin attained complete *hesychia* by the grace of God and by her way of life.[29] As Metropolitan Kallistos puts it, she was "transfigured by the divine light" and "saw the uncreated God reflected in the purity of her heart as in a mirror."[30]

---

[26]Rt. Revd. Kallistos of Diokleia, "The Feast of Mary's Silence: The Entry into the Temple (21 Nov.)," in A. Stacpoole, ed., *Mary in Doctrine and Devotion. Papers of the Liverpool Congress, 1989, of the Ecumenical Society of the Blessed Virgin Mary* (Dublin: The Columba Press, 1990), 34–41.

[27]Christopher Veniamin, trans., *St Gregory Palamas. The Homilies* (Waymart, PA: Mt Thabor Publishing, 2009), Homily 53, 414–44.

[28]Rt. Revd. Kallistos, "The Feast of Mary's silence," 39.

[29]*St Gregory Palamas, The Homilies*, Homily 53, 441–42.

[30]Rt. Revd. Kallistos, "The Feast of Mary's Silence," 39.

This hesychastic image of the Mother of God is not new in Orthodox tradition; as we saw in Chapter Four, monastic writers including the fourth-century Athanasius of Alexandria pictured Mary
as a pious virgin who was engaged in a life of ascetic training and
prayer. Gregory Palamas took the idea further in portraying her
as one who attained the highest level of mystical communion with
God; this enabled her to hear his message at the Annunciation and
to join her flesh with him. Metropolitan Kallistos reminds us both
of Mary's humanity and of her special qualities, as virgin, mystic,
and Mother of God.

Mary as Church

One other modern approach to the Mother of God that is worthy of note is a chapter in Father John Behr's short book, *The
Mystery of Christ. Life in Death.*[31] In examining Mary's virginity
and motherhood of Christ, Behr takes us back to some second-
and third-century sources that explore the symbolic meaning of
Mary's role. Writers in this period were fond of framing their
theological ideas in allegorical terms: this is a mode of discourse
that many modern Christians have forgotten or find difficult to
understand. Theological meaning is more important than histo-
ricity in such contexts, as we have already seen in the case of texts
such as the *Protevangelium of James.*

Many early Christian writers pictured the Church, which God
founded before the rest of creation, as a female figure—and
indeed, sometimes as a Virgin Mother. The late-second-century
Letter of the Churches of Vienne and Lyons, for example, writes

---

[31] J. Behr, *The Mystery of Christ. Life in Death* (Crestwood, NY: St Vladimir's
Seminary Press, 2006).

of the Church as follows, in the course of a narrative about the execution in the arena of a group of Christians:

> Through their continued life the dead were made alive, and the witnesses (martyrs) showed favor to those who had failed to witness. And there was great joy for the Virgin Mother in receiving back alive those whom she had miscarried as dead. For through them the majority of those who had denied were again conceived and again brought to life and learned to confess; and now living and strengthened, they went to the judgment seat.[32]

In this text, "Virgin Mother" clearly refers to the Church, which is envisaged as a cosmic personification who receives back the souls of those who have surrendered their earthly lives in their witness to Christ. Eventually this image would be conflated with Mary, the Mother of God, who symbolically represents the mother who gave us all birth into the life of God and continues to nourish us with spiritual milk and protection.[33] Such complex symbolism, in which two allegorical figures interact and eventually become one, may seem foreign to modern Christians. However, as Behr points out, such interpretations enrich our apprehension of Mary's importance in the Christian dispensation.

As Orthodox liturgical texts make clear throughout the ecclesiastical year, the Mother of God represents the whole of humanity and, by implication, the Church. She is the one who accepted God's will and allowed him to enter creation as the Incarnate

[32]Behr, *The Mystery of Christ*, 121–22, quoting Eusebius, *Ecclesiastical History* 5.1.45–6.

[33]See, for example, Clement of Alexandria, *Paedagogus* 1.6, quoted in Behr, *The Mystery of Christ*, 123–4.

Christ. She is the Bride who was prepared and ready to meet Christ, her Bridegroom. Orthodox Christians invoke Christ with her mediation: like a mother, she watches over Christians and helps them to grow in the life of Christ. The identification of Mary with the Church represents even more than this, however, in its ontological reality. The Mother of God is the earthly and physical place that God entered and where he is nourished and brought to birth. In the same way, the Church, made up of human beings who have become one with the body of Christ through baptism and the Eucharist, experiences God's presence in liturgical celebration and daily life. As Father John Behr makes clear, with the help of types and images drawn from early Christian sources, the image of the Virgin Mary as Church is one of the oldest and most meaningful ways in which her mysterious role has been expressed.

Conclusion

In this chapter we have explored various themes that have appeared in the writings of modern Orthodox theologians and preachers. Some important figures have been omitted for reasons of space: a whole book on modern Orthodox Mariological thought would clearly be desirable in future. In focusing on the themes that I selected for discussion, including the Virgin Mary's role as "Wisdom," feminine principle, created being, model for humankind, "silence," and Church, it is clear that a variety of sources have provided scholars and teachers with inspiration. These include Scripture (including both Old and New Testaments), the apocrypha, Greek (especially Platonic) philosophy, and the writings of the Fathers. Nothing is entirely new in Orthodox Christian theology, but thinkers throughout the ages have delighted in putting together ideas or images in new ways.

It is worth reiterating here some of the features of Orthodox thought that are held in common by all of the writers that we have examined and which distinguish them from aspects of Western Christian Mariology. Firstly, it is noteworthy that every Orthodox thinker works from a basis of liturgical life in the Church and active prayer. As Behr-Sigel points out, the Orthodox Church has always avoided making dogmatic statements about the Mother of God, apart from accepting the affirmation of her role as Theotokos at the council of Ephesus in AD 431. Rather, it "prefers to teach and initiate the faithful progressively to this mystery by using the images and symbols of liturgical poetry rather than the restricting conceptual approach."[34] Secondly, Orthodox writers uniformly insist on Mary's humanity, as witnessed in her ordinary (although miraculous) birth, experience of doubt and sorrow as well as motherly tenderness, and genuine death. It is true that, according to tradition, the Mother of God was assumed into heaven in body and soul, thus allowing her resurrection before the Final Day, but even in this state of glory she remains united in nature with the rest of humankind. Thirdly, as we have seen, Orthodox writers tend to speak of the Mother of God by means of typological and poetic imagery rather than in discursive language. As all of the theologians covered in this chapter agree, Mary is surrounded by mystery: her life was shrouded in silence for several centuries after her death; she spoke rarely, according to both Biblical and apocryphal sources; and her role in the Incarnation remains a deep mystery that is beyond human comprehension. It is these considerations, as we shall see in the following chapter, that make communication between Orthodox and Western (both Roman Catholic and Protestant) Christians difficult at times, even

[34]Behr-Sigel, *The Ministry of Women in the Church*, 214.

though there is in fact considerable common ground between the various confessions.

Further Reading:

Behr, John. *The Mystery of Christ. Life in Death.* Crestwood, NY: St Vladimir's Seminary Press, 2006.

Behr-Sigel, Elisabeth. *The Ministry of Women in the Church,* trans. S. Bigham, esp. Chapter Six: "Mary, the Mother of God: Traditional Mariology and New Questions." Redondo Beach, CA: Oakwood Publications, 1991.

Bulgakov, Sergei. *The Bride of the Lamb,* trans. B. Jakim. Edinburgh: T. & T. Clark, 2002.

Bulgakov, Sergei. *The Burning Bush. On the Orthodox Veneration of the Mother of God,* trans. T.A. Smith. Grand Rapids, MI and Cambridge: William Eerdmans Publishing Co., 2009.

Evdokimov, Paul. *Woman and the Salvation of the World. A Christian Anthropology on the Charisms of Women,* trans. A.P. Gythiel. Crestwood, NY: St Vladimir's Seminary Press, 1994.

Louth, Andrew. "Father Sergii Bulgakov on the Mother of God." *St Vladimir's Theological Quarterly* 49: 1–2 (2005), 145–64.

Robinson, Wendy. "Mary: The Flower and Fruit of Worship: The Mother of God in the Orthodox Tradition," in J. Behr, A. Louth, and D. Conomos, eds. *Abba: The Tradition of Orthodoxy in the West. Festschrift for Bishop Kallistos (Ware) of Diokleia.* Crestwood, NY: St Vladimir's Seminary Press, 2003, 193–205.

[Ware] Kallistos, His Eminence, Metropolitan of Diokleia. "The Feast of Mary's Silence: The Entry into the Temple (21 Nov.)," in A. Stacpoole, ed., *Mary in Doctrine and Devotion. Papers of the Liverpool Congress, 1989, of the Ecumenical Society of the Blessed Virgin Mary.* Dublin: The Columba Press, 34–41.

chapter eight
THE VIRGIN MARY AND ECUMENISM

M any Christian Churches share a deep devotion to the Mary, the Mother of God. It is true, of course, that some Protestants see such veneration as non-biblical and as a distraction from worship of the Holy Trinity. However, respect for the Virgin Mary may be present even if a more devotional attitude is avoided. As the mother of Jesus, the Virgin Mary will always play a central role in the Christian narrative and its theological exegesis.

It is also worth noting that the Islamic faith holds the Virgin Mary in high regard. The Qur'an honors her as the mother of the prophet Jesus, affirming that she was a virgin at the time of his conception. At the scene of the Annunciation, angels address Mary with the words, "O Mary! God has chosen you and purified you; He has chosen you above all women!"[1] Some Muslims regularly visit Marian shrines in Turkey or the Near East and some, especially Shi'a groups, accept as part of their tradition the story of Mary's infancy in the temple, during which she grew

---

[1]*Sura* III.38; A.J. Arberry, trans., *The Koran Interpreted* (Oxford: Oxford University Press, 1982), 51 (with adjustments).

in holiness.[2] There is also evidence, in spite of a long history of polemic between Jews and Christians on the subject of the Virgin Mary,[3] that some Jewish thinkers wish to reclaim her as a model of motherhood and godliness.[4] Because of her relationship with Jesus, her son, and on account of her pious conduct, the Virgin Mary thus represents a significant figure for adherents of all three Abrahamic religions.

We should not minimize, however, the differences that exist in the various views of the Virgin Mary. For our purposes, the most important variations are those between Roman Catholic and Orthodox teachings—mainly because these two traditions remain close to each other in their faithful veneration of the Theotokos throughout many centuries and in their belief in her importance in the mystery of the Incarnation. The dogmatic differences, which have been highlighted at various points in the course of this book, include the understanding of Mary's relationship with the rest of humanity—especially with regard to "original" or "ancestral"

---

[2]T. Khalidi, ed. and trans., *The Muslim Jesus. Sayings and Stories in Isalmic Literature* (Cambridge, MA and London: Harvard University Press, 2003, esp. 196–7.

[3]The earliest evidence for such debate can be found in Justin Martyr's *Dialogue with Trypho* 63–70, trans. T.B. Falls, *St Justin Martyr. Dialogue with Trypho* (Washington, DC: The Catholic University of America Press, 2003), 97–110. A later debate, which propounds the Jewish point of view, can be found in the ninth-century text known as *The Polemic of Nestor the Priest*, ed. D.J. Lasker, S. Stroumsa, and J. Niehoff-Panagiotidis (Jerusalem: Ben-Zvi Institute for the Study of Jewish Communities, 1996).

[4]See, for example, Dominique Cerbelaud, OP, "The Virgin Mary, A Jewish Woman," in W. McLoughlin and J. Pinnock, eds., *Mary For Time and Eternity. Essays on Mary and Ecumenism* (Leominster: Gracewing, 2007), 289–97.

sin—and the nature of her death (Dormition) and Assumption into heaven. Although the Catholic and Orthodox positions do not in fact differ significantly, especially with regard to Mary's Assumption, there has always been unease in Orthodox circles with the extent to which Catholic theologians have sought to define Marian doctrine too systematically—especially in linking her Assumption with her Immaculate Conception (on which, see below). Orthodox preachers and writers prefer this matter to remain mysterious; without building on the doctrine that was expressed at the council of Ephesus in 431, they accept the Marian liturgical and exegetical traditions that have developed gradually in the life of the Church.

In this chapter, we will look first at Roman Catholic tradition and its teachings about the Virgin Mary. After doctrinal, liturgical, and hagiographical developments that were deeply influenced by the Eastern, Byzantine tradition, dogmatic ideas, especially concerning the Virgin Mary's "Immaculate Conception," appeared only from the eleventh century onward, and they were debated for centuries before being accepted in the papal bull, *Ineffabilis Deus,* of 1854. This teaching, along with that on the Virgin's Assumption into heaven (expressed in a papal bull in 1950), has caused concern to modern Orthodox theologians. We will therefore examine this question carefully, attempting to understand its significance in theological terms. Finally, however, it is worth reminding ourselves of recent attempts, in the ecumenical sphere, for better understanding and appreciation of what both traditions share in their veneration of the Mother of God.

Early Veneration of the Mother of God in East and West

As we have seen in earlier chapters of this book, devotion to the Virgin Mary emerged throughout the universal Church in the first millennium after Christ. After an initial period of relative silence, theologians from the fourth century onward began to celebrate Mary's essential role in the Incarnation, as well as her personal purity and piety, in both East and West. In the Latin-speaking half of Christendom, bishops including Ambrose of Milan and Augustine of Hippo wrote sermons and treatises in which they extolled Mary's virginity and motherhood of God. Although dissenting voices occasionally challenged aspects of Mary's exaltation, it appears that, as in the East, the Roman Church accepted her Christological importance and veneration.[5] Before the sixth century, Western attention focused mainly on the Virgin Mary's relationship with Christ and to the Church, with some writers also praising her ascetic way of life and virginal purity.

From about the late sixth century onward, miracle stories involving Mary also began to circulate in Western Europe.[6] She took on the role of protector and intercessor here at about the same time that this began to be celebrated in Constantinople. It is also worth noting that Marian feast-days were transferred to the calendar of the Western Church soon after being introduced in Constantinople between about the middle of the sixth and eighth centuries. The most problematic of these festivals, from the point of view

[5]See above, Chapter Six, pp. 139–40.

[6]See especially Gregory of Tours, extracts in L. Gambero, ed., *Mary and the Fathers of the Church. The Blessed Virgin Mary in Patristic Thought* (San Francisco, CA: Ignatius Press, 1999), 352–58.

of some Western Church leaders, was that of St Anna's Conception of Mary (December 8),[7] which was first introduced into the Western liturgical cycle in the ninth century but spread to England and France in the eleventh and twelfth centuries, respectively. The reason that this feast caused controversy was that it seemed to support a new doctrine concerning Mary, that of the "Immaculate Conception."

The doctrine of the Immaculate Conception

The idea that Mary, the Birth-giver of God, must herself be free of any taint of human sinfulness appeared first in Northern Europe—especially in Anglo-Saxon England where Marian devotion had always been strong.[8] From the early twelfth through the fourteenth centuries, medieval theologians debated this new idea. It is interesting to note that in addition to having strong support in England, the doctrine was promoted especially by members of religious orders such as the Franciscans and the Carmelites. Its opponents, on the other hand, came from the Benedictine and Dominican orders, with figures such as Bernard of Clairvaux and Thomas Aquinas arguing against it on both biblical and theological grounds. This is not to say that the latter opposed Mary's important role in the Incarnation of Christ or that they did not venerate her as a holy figure. Many of these thinkers, including

[7]The feast is celebrated on December 9 in the Eastern Churches, but on the previous day in the West.

[8]See Mary Clayton, *The Cult of the Virgin in Anglo-Saxon England* (Cambridge: Cambridge University Press, 1990). Some of the main defenders of the doctrine of the Immaculate Conception during the Middle Ages were English. They include Eadmer of Canterbury, William of Ware, and John Duns Scotus.

especially Bernard, produced theological—even highly mystical—writings in honor of Mary.[9] However, the opponents of the doctrine argued that, in addition to having no basis in Scripture or tradition, the doctrine undermines her links with the rest of humanity.

This controversy rumbled on for centuries in the West. It was discussed at the council of Basel in 1439, where the dogma was formally accepted for the first time. However, this council lacked political and legal backing, especially from Rome, so the decree had limited impact in the Catholic Church. The Council of Trent (1545–63) carefully avoided the subject in its discussion of original sin, but belief in the Virgin Mary's Immaculate Conception gained increasing acceptance—even among Dominicans—in the centuries that followed. Finally, and possibly as a result of popular pressure, Pope Pius IX published the *Ineffabilis Deus* in 1854. This bull proclaimed that God elected Mary pre-eternally to be Mother of God. It is for this reason that—in this case alone among all human beings—Christ the Savior absolved her from any taint of sinfulness even before her conception. The doctrine thus sets the Virgin Mary apart from the rest of humanity in her freedom from original sin, that is, the fallen condition that can be traced back to Adam and Eve.

It is worth pausing at this point to discuss what Roman Catholic tradition means by "original sin." If Mary is said never to have

---

[9]See, for example, Bernard of Clairvaux's Marian sermons, translated in M.-B. Saïd and G. Perigo, *Magnificat: Homilies in Praise of the Blessed Virgin Mary*, Cistercian Fathers Series 18 (Kalamazoo, MI: Cistercian Publications, 1979); L. Gambero, *Mary in the Middle Ages. The Blessed Virgin Mary in the Thought of the Medieval Latin Theologians*, trans. T. Buffer (San Francisco: Ignatius Press, 2000), 234–42.

experienced this condition, then we need to understand exactly what it entails. Although the Orthodox and Western Christian traditions both accept that the fall from grace that is described in the third chapter of Genesis had momentous consequences for humanity, they do not interpret this catastrophe in quite the same way. In the West, especially since Augustine of Hippo's writings on the subject in the early fifth century, original sin has been understood as a tendency to disobey God that is passed on at the moment of conception. It is associated with sexual reproduction, which is itself a product of the fall and it also involves feelings of selfishness and guilt. Such innate sinfulness is washed away in baptism, but human beings continue even after this saving sacrament to be assailed by concupiscence—that is, the desire to submit to passions that may be self-serving or destructive.[10]

The Virgin Mary, having been preserved completely from the consequences of the fall, is thus believed by Roman Catholics free not only from sin, but even from temptation. The doctrine of the Immaculate Conception leads Catholic theologians to wrestle with the meaning of Symeon's prophecy that a sword would "pierce through [Mary's] soul" or with the problem of the Virgin's feelings of doubt at the Annunciation and grief at the Cross.[11] The dogma of the Immaculate Conception thus departs in significant ways from the Patristic and medieval traditions in both East and West. The Orthodox Church has opposed the pronouncement

[10]See *Catechism of the Catholic Church* (London: Geoffrey Chapman, 1994), 286.

[11]See, for example, A. Agius, "The Problem of Mary's Holiness in the First Christian Centuries," *Marian Studies* 14 (1963), 41–61; D. McCracken, *The Scandal of the Gospels: Jesus, Story, and Offense* (New York: Oxford University Press, 1994).

since its promulgation in 1854 for a number of reasons, which we shall now take the time to examine.

Orthodox Christian objections to the Doctrine of the Immaculate Conception

It is important to emphasize first that Orthodox Christian arguments against this dogma are varied and that they do not all carry equal weight. We can dismiss immediately, for example, the idea that the dogma is heretical simply by virtue of having been defined by the Pope. This position is indefensible on logical grounds since Roman Popes have, undeniably, expressed many ideas that are orthodox in the course of the last millennium (or since the schism of 1054). More fundamental, however, is the view that the Pope should not express new doctrines relating to Christian faith without the summoning of an ecumenical council. This criticism can be leveled not only at the papal bulls of 1854 and 1950, regarding the Virgin Mary, but also at every other decision, such as the acceptance of the *filioque* clause, that has been reached without the agreement of the universal Church.

Second, the Orthodox Churches object to a doctrine that, by preserving the Mother of God from the normal human condition, results in her separation from the rest of humanity. This separation can be seen to operate on two levels: in the first place, Mary becomes someone whose physical nature is in some way different from that of all other mortals. If she has been preserved from our shared and innate tendency to sin, can we actually say that she shares fully our fallen human nature? Then, on a moral level, we begin to see problems relating to Mary's intellectual and emotional experiences in this world. Some Roman Catholic theologians question whether she experienced doubt, pain or sorrow, if she were immune to the inner turmoil that afflicts all other human beings.[12] Orthodox thinkers, from the early centuries onward, have, as we have seen earlier in this book, acknowledged Mary's susceptibility to all of these emotions. Some, like Athanasius of Alexandria, picture her growing slowly in understanding and holiness, with the help of the Holy Spirit.[13] More fundamentally, and keeping with both of the aspects of the Virgin's being that we have just seen, Orthodox Christological doctrine emphasizes her—and by extension, Christ's—full participation in the human condition. As Gregory Nazianzen put it, "God has come to suffer in the way that we suffer, by becoming human, and has endured the poverty of being constituted as flesh, 'so that we might become rich by his poverty'" (2 Cor 8.9).[14] Mary, the Mother of God, provided Christ with the human nature in which he fully experienced every aspect of human life including death. If she is removed entirely from the sphere of the fallen world in which we live, then the link between creation and divine being in the mystery of the Incarnation is lost.

A key aspect of this debate clearly lies in the difference between Eastern and Western understandings of "original" or "ancestral"

---

[12]St Paul describes this condition vividly in Romans 7.15: "For what I am doing, I do not understand. For what I will to do, that I do not practise; but what I hate, that I do."

[13]Athanasius of Alexandria, *Letters to the Virgins*, trans. D. Brakke, *Athanasius and Asceticism* (Baltimore and London: John Hopkins University Press, 1995), 274–302.

[14]Gregory of Nazianzus, *Oration 44 "For New Sunday"* 4, trans. B.E. Daley, S.J., *Gregory of Nazianzus* (London and New York: Routledge, 2006), 157.

sin. It would be inaccurate to say that the Orthodox Church has no concept of original sin; on the contrary, the belief that we have lived in a fallen world and had a tendency to sin since our first parents' disastrous choice in paradise (Gen 3.6) is as strong in the Greek as in the Latin tradition. There are some differences, however, which have influenced the responses of each Church to this problem. Whereas the Catholic tradition has, since Augustine of Hippo, emphasized an innate guilty state that is inherited by every human being, the Eastern Church has stressed the fact that whereas we have a *tendency* to sin, we are responsible for our actions and may, from the moment that we attain a rational sense of our free will, either turn away or towards God. Maximus the Confessor distinguished between "natural" and "gnomic" will: the former, which is inherited, may mean that we are likely to sin, but a sinful act can only be undertaken with the gnomic will, or in other words, the free decision to follow our appetitive instincts or passions.

It is such different understandings of the meaning of original, or ancestral, sin that cause a divide in Eastern and Western views of the Virgin Mary's personal condition. For Western theologians, Mary would share the inherited guilt of Adam's and Eve's dis-obedience if Christ, the Savior, had not prevented this before she was even conceived. For Eastern thinkers, the Virgin shares in our inherited ability, concomitant with the gift of free will, to choose between good and evil. If we remove this freedom of choice, then Mary's decision to obey God at the Annunciation loses its signifi-cance. Her choice on this momentous occasion became the para-digm, in both existential and moral terms, of human acceptance of God's purpose and love for his creation.

The Dormition and Assumption as Ecumenical Issues

Another aspect of Christian belief concerning Mary, the Mother of God, is her death and Assumption into heaven, as recounted in numerous apocryphal texts dating from the end of the fifth century onward. Both Eastern and Western Churches accepted versions of these narratives as holy tradition and, from the late sixth century onward, instituted a feast on August 15 to celebrate the event. Homilies and hymns were written and icons were painted in its honor as Christians meditated on the meaning of Mary's miraculous disappearance from her tomb after three days and her bodily translation into heaven. The main difference between Orthodox and Catholic interpretations of the Dormition, at least from the late Middle Ages onward, has been that whereas Orthodox thinkers prefer not to delve too deeply into what is regarded as an ineffable mystery, Scholastic theologians in the West have explored its theological implications and have linked it with her Immaculate Conception. It is perhaps a result of the doctrine's lack of firm definition that led Pope Pius XII, to publish an "apostolic constitution" known as the *Munificentissimus Deus* on November 1, 1950 in which its meaning was elucidated and a new Mass was provided for the feast.[15]

Orthodox and Catholic understandings of the Dormition and Assumption of the Virgin Mary are in fact much closer to each other than are their views of her Immaculate Conception. The two traditions both accept the apocryphal narratives that underpin this doctrine, even if the particular stories that they accept may vary in certain details. Nevertheless, the publication of the 1950

---

[15]Extracts of the text can be found in S.J. Boss, ed., *Mary: The Complete Resource* (London and New York: Continuum, 2007), 281–83.

constitution caused as much dismay in Orthodox circles as did that of 1854. The view that the Pope should not express doctrinal statements without the authority of an ecumenical council applies to both cases. In addition to this, however, Orthodox critics have felt that the papal pronouncement reduces a topic that is shrouded in mystery to a formulaic statement. As Andrew of Crete, John of Damascus, and Germanus of Constantinople all recognized when preaching on this subject in the eighth century, it is mysterious and ineffable. They, like other Byzantine and later Orthodox writers, preferred to use metaphors and euphemisms to describe Mary's afterlife, not to discuss its meaning in discursive language.[16] The papal *Munificentissimus Deus*, however, states clearly that the Virgin Mary, "having completed the course of her earthly life, was assumed body and soul into heavenly glory."[17]

Perhaps the most striking difference between the two traditions lies in their manner of describing the glorious death and assumption of the Mother of God. Whereas Byzantine, Russian and other Orthodox iconographical traditions portray Mary's modest "falling asleep," or death, in the midst of the apostles, with Christ receiving her soul which resembles a swaddled infant, Western paintings depict her ascending, often magnificently dressed and surrounded by angels, into heaven. Another related image that is beloved by Western artists is the scene of the Virgin's coronation by Christ in heaven: she is pictured as sitting in majesty with him, along with the Father and the Holy Spirit.

[16]See Brian Daley's useful discussion of the approach followed by these liturgical writers in *On the Dormition of Mary. Early Patristic Homilies* (Crestwood, NY: St Vladimir's Seminary Press, 1998), 28–34.

[17]*Munificentissimus Deus* 44, trans. Boss, *Mary: The Complete Resource*, 283.

Having highlighted these differences in art, however, it is worth emphasizing that the liturgical and literary treatment of Mary's Assumption is not so very different in East and West. Byzantine homilies on the feast of the Dormition invoke her in high-flown terms as "Ever-Virgin," "Heavenly Queen," and "Mother of God." Is this so very different from the language that appears in the papal pronouncements, as they extol her glory in connection with her Assumption into heaven? In both traditions, Mary is pictured as interceding with her Son, the Righteous Judge, on behalf of humanity. The only real divergences between doctrinal stances, in the final analysis, lies in the Roman Catholic desire to elucidate the doctrine surrounding these events as opposed to the Orthodox preference for mystery that is beyond explanation.

Mutual Cooperation and Discussion Between the Churches

It is worth pointing out, before we move on to explore recent discussions between Christian leaders and thinkers of various Churches, that cooperation has already been occurring in a quiet way between scholars within these traditions for several centuries. We owe much to Bollandist, Assumptionist, and Jesuit scholars, for example, for their meticulous editions and studies of Greek liturgical and hagiographical texts. In the twentieth century, scholars such as Martin Jugie, Antoine Wenger, and Simon Mimouni have helped to elucidate the complicated literary traditions that surround the Virgin Mary's death and Assumption into heaven. Jugie, who sought to justify the papal decisions of both 1854 and 1950 by means of rigorous textual analysis, was convinced that the Orthodox and Catholic positions regarding

Mary's Immaculate Conception and Assumption were not so far apart after all.[18] It is also significant, as he himself remarked, that justification for the doctrine of the Immaculate Conception lies primarily in the work of the Greek Fathers, who continually proclaimed her virginal purity and freedom from sin. Where they would have disagreed with his argument, however, was his premise that "sinlessness" implies a complete absence of the inherited *ability to sin* that goes with human nature. Other Roman Catholics who have opened up the treasures of the Orthodox Christian liturgical tradition to a wider scholarly audience include the late Michel van Esbroeck, Michel Aubineau, and many others. Such appreciation of Orthodox Mariology must rest on a basis of common belief: these scholars have, from the beginnings of the revival of patristic studies in the seventeenth century, recognized that all Christians share a common heritage in the Eastern and Western traditions.

In more recent years, various ecumenical groups have emerged, some of which are specifically concerned with Marian doctrine and devotion. The Ecumenical Society of the Blessed Virgin Mary, for example, has hosted conferences and published their proceedings. Numerous other publications, combining studies by Christians and even members of other faiths, continue to appear at a bewildering rate. What they all bear witness to, in their diversity and abundance, is both the enduring popularity of the subject and its witness to God's ongoing relationship with his creation.

---

[18]M. Jugie, *La mort et l'assomption de la sainte Vierge. Étude historico-doctrinale*, Studi e Testi 114 (Vatican City: Biblioteca Apostolica Vaticana, 1944); idem, *L'immaculée conception dans l'écriture sainte et dans la tradition orientale*, Bibliotheca Immaculatae Conceptionis 3 (Rome: Officium Libri Catholici, 1952).

The more ecumenically-minded books are, needless to say, eirenic in tone and respectful of differences between Orthodox, Roman Catholic, and Protestant positions. At the same time, they show no tendency to explain away real differences in these traditions. It is possible to say that, at least at the scholarly level, discussions concerning the Mother of God between adherents of various Churches are ongoing, fruitful, and enlightened.

At a more official level, however, things are perhaps not quite so relaxed. This is probably because the ordained leaders of the various Churches accept their responsibility to uphold orthodoxy as they understand it. The issue of hierarchical power, which is sometimes influenced by political considerations, may also play a part. One other ongoing problem is the lack of an appropriate ecclesiastical context in which such discussions might take place. Ecumenical councils remain impossible as long as official schism persists—quite apart from the question whether it is appropriate to go on discussing matters of Christian doctrine in such a context—and, judging by the experience of the council at Ferrara-Florence in 1438–39, the logistics and protocol of such a meeting would be daunting. In my view, it is more likely that discussions between the Eastern and Western Churches concerning Mary, the Mother of God, will continue at the popular or scholarly levels. In this way, as in the past, our understanding of the ways in which Catholic, Orthodox, and other perceptions of the Virgin Mary overlap will grow slowly in the quiet settings that suit this holy figure. Above all, it is the liturgical and spiritual traditions in Christianity that reveal who she is and how she relates both to us, the human members of the Church, and to the Trinitarian God.

Further Reading:

Boss, Sarah Jane. *Mary: The Complete Resource.* London and New York: Continuum, 2007.

Cunningham, Mary B. " 'All-holy Infant': Byzantine and Western Views on the Conception of the Virgin Mary." *St Vladimir's Theological Quarterly* 50, nos. 1–2 (2006), 127–48.

McHugh, Canon John. "The Doctrine of the Immaculate Conception: Reflections on a Problem in Ecumenical Dialogue," in A. Stacpoole, ed. *Mary in Doctrine and Devotion. Papers of the Liverpool Congress, 1989, of the Ecumenical Society of the Blessed Virgin Mary.* Dublin: The Columba Press, 1990, 23–33.

McLoughlin, W. and J. Pinnock, eds. *Mary For Time and Eternity. Essays on Mary and Ecumenism.* Leominster: Gracewing, 2007.

Shoemaker, Stephen. *Ancient Traditions of the Virgin Mary's Dormition and Assumption.* Oxford: Oxford University Press, 2002.

CONCLUSION

When you take the word of Christ and shape it in your mind and transform it in your thought as if in a womb, you are called his mother.[1]

As we have seen throughout this book, the Virgin Mary, Mother of God, is a central figure in Orthodox Christian tradition. She is a powerful symbol of the Incarnation, as witnessed by many types in the Old Testament and poetic images that have become associated with her in the course of centuries. As liturgical texts make clear, Mary acted as the receptacle that received and nurtured Christ when, as God-man, he entered his own creation. She was also a very human figure, following her Son in his ministry and weeping for him at the Cross. For Orthodox Christians, Mary represents both themselves, in their receptivity to salvation in Christ, and collectively, the Church who awaits him as her Bridegroom. And, in addition to these roles, the Mother of God acts as intercessor for Christians: in this sense she is everyone's mother, helping, protecting, and mediating on their behalf before God, the All-Ruler and Righteous Judge. As Orthodox Christians say, towards the end of their morning prayers, each day:

[1]Severian of Gabala, *De caeco et Zacchaeo*, PG 59, 605.

All my hope I place in you, Mother of God; guard me under your protection.[2]

Although an awareness of Mary's many roles may have been nascent in the earliest Church, the apostolic and post-apostolic Fathers were slow to write about her Christological and intercessory importance. Later Orthodox writers have sought to explain this silence, suggesting—quite convincingly—that early Christians respected the mystery that surrounded Christ's mother. As we saw in Chapter Four, Ignatius of Antioch wrote that Mary's virginity and birth-giving, along with the Passion of Christ, took place "in the deep silence of the Lord."[3]

Slowly, as time passed, stories and theological discussion concerning the Virgin Mary began to be produced. By the end of the fifth century, Christians were informed about her parents, upbringing, death, and translation into heaven; those who were able to assimilate the doctrine that was formulated at the councils of Ephesus and Chalcedon also knew that she had borne God—the Divine Son—in her womb. Somewhat later, and certainly by the beginning of the seventh century, Constantinopolitan Christians were addressing Mary as their city's defender and intercessor. She was seen fighting on the walls during the siege by Persians and Avars in 626 and was credited with having sunk their boats and driven them away.

---

[2]Archimandrite Ephrem Lash, trans., *An Orthodox Prayer Book* (Oxford: Oxford University Press, 1999), 10.

[3]See above, pp. 93–4. Ignatius of Antioch, *Letter to the Ephesians* 19, trans. M. Staniforth, *Early Christian Writings: The Apostolic Fathers* (London: Penguin, 1968), 66.

It is in the Middle Byzantine period (approximately AD 600 to 1204) that liturgical texts, including especially the hymns that adorn the great feasts and the offices for each day of the year, were composed and included in books such as the *Menaion*, the *Octoechos*, the *Triodion*, and many others. These texts remain the clearest expression of the Orthodox Church's view of the Mother of God. The ancient assertion that *lex orandi est lex credendi* (which could be paraphrased, "as we pray, so we believe") is especially applicable to the place of Mary in this tradition.[4] Silence continues to surround Mary, at least with regard to the doctrinal definition of her nature, as virginal mother and intercessor. At the same time, however, she is praised in many words, most of which allude mysteriously and poetically to her central role in the Incarnation. Mary resides at the heart of Orthodox Christian worship, as the many *theotokia* and invocations that are scattered throughout the liturgical offices make clear. Her role as bridge between God and his creation, in giving birth to the incarnate Christ, is carefully balanced in such hymns with recognition of her protective love for the rest of humanity.

While I have attempted throughout this book to describe both the historical development and liturgical expression of Mary's role in Orthodox Christian tradition, I am all too aware of the topics which, for reasons of space, I have left out. It would have been useful, for example, to describe in more detail the theological and scriptural content of individual Marian feasts. Another

---

[4]Father Alexander Schmemann promoted this principle, which appeared originally in the writings of Prosper of Acquitaine. See A. Schmemann, *Introduction to Liturgical Theology*, trans. A.E. Moorhouse (Leighton Buzzard: The Faith Press, 1966; repr. Crestwood, NY: St Vladimir's Seminary Press, 1975), 15; Prosper of Aquitaine, PL 51, cols. 209–10.

subject that merits detailed study, but which has been examined elsewhere in studies on holy icons, is the variety of iconographical types, such as the Virgin "Hodegetria" ("Who guides"), "Orans" ("Who prays" or is a "Sign"), "Eleousa" ("Who is merciful" or "Who is tender"), "Glykophilousa" ("Who is sweetly-loving"), and others. Such icons enable Christians to meditate on the different aspects of Mary's being and role in the Church.[5] Many other material objects, dating from the Byzantine through the modern period, offer access to the Mother of God by means of their imagery and usage.[6] This book has focused for the most part on texts, but those who wish to pursue their study of Mary's place in Orthodox Christian tradition should be aware that she is honored in many media, including icons, paintings, precious objects, music, and architecture.

So what special contribution does Orthodox Christian tradition make to the rich and varied tapestry of Marian doctrine and devotion? The emphasis on Mary's humanity, as well as on her physical connection with the whole of creation, is one of the most striking aspects of Orthodox celebration of this holy figure. This is well illustrated by a passage from the *Akathistos Hymn*, which, as we have seen above, is one of the oldest liturgical texts concerning Mary and which is sung annually during Lent. Ikos seven, in its entirety, reads as follows:

[5]For a good introduction to this subject, see L. Ouspensky and V. Lossky, *The Meaning of Icons* (Crestwood, NY: St Vladimir's Seminary Press, 1983), 76–103; R. Williams, *Ponder These Things. Praying with Icons of the Virgin* (Norwich: The Canterbury Press, 2002).

[6]For discussion and photographs of the Byzantine material, see the catalogue of the splendid exhibition that was held at the Benaki Museum, Athens, in 2000: M. Vassilaki, ed., *Mother of God. Representations of the Virgin in Byzantine Art* (Milan: Skira, 2000).

A new creation has the Creator revealed, manifesting himself unto us his creatures. From a Virgin's womb he came, preserving it inviolate as it was before: that, beholding the miracle, we might sing her praises, crying:

Hail, flower of incorruption:
Hail, crown of chastity.
Hail, bright foreshadowing of resurrection glory:
Hail, mirror of the angels' life.
Hail, tree of glorious fruit on which the faithful feed:
Hail, wood of shady leaves where many shelter.
Hail, for you have conceived a Guide for the wanderers:
Hail, for you have borne a Deliverer for the captives.
Hail, intercessor with the Righteous Judge:
Hail, forgiveness for many who have stumbled.
Hail, robe for the naked and bereft of hope:
Hail, love surpassing all desire.
Hail, Bride without a bridegroom![7]

By means of metaphor and poetic imagery, this hymn reminds listeners of every theological aspect of Mary, the Mother of God. She is the Virgin who gave birth to God; she is intercessor before the Righteous Judge. However, Mary is also linked decisively with creation in her identification with the "wood of shady leaves where many shelter." Orthodox liturgical poetry succeeds in weaving together many layers of meaning in passages such as this: Mary is also identified with the tree of knowledge from which the faithful *should* eat, thereby recapitulating the original tree by which they fell from grace.

[7]Mother Mary and Archimandrite Kallistos Ware, trans., *The Lenten Triodion* (London and Boston: Faber and Faber, 1978; repr. S. Canaan, PA: St Tikhon's Seminary Press, 2002), 428–29 (with adjustments).

Images of nature, daily life, and Biblical types (which are also frequently symbolic of creation) run through both hymns and homilies that celebrate the Mother of God. At the same time, this imagery evokes a transfigured creation: this is the natural world in which God himself is immanent. It is not surprising that, in addition to liturgical poetry, Orthodox literature and art express the Church's love for the Mother of God. Novelists such as Fyodor Dostoevsky and Anton Chekhov refer to her frequently—sometimes through the voices of their characters—because her presence was so firmly embedded in nineteenth-century Russian culture. Mary embodies the paradox that lies at the heart of Orthodox Christology: she represents both humanity and creation—in all their complexity— but she also contains the God who has emptied himself in order to enter into these fully. By means of liturgical poetry, narrative, and art, the Church defines Mary as that holy but richly diverse place where divinity and humanity come together.

While Orthodox Christian tradition has been especially effective in emphasizing Mary's humanity and ongoing link with creation, it overlaps in many ways with other Christian traditions, especially the Roman Catholic, in its praise of her glory as Mother of God. It is important to celebrate what these confessions share. With respect to Mariology, it should be remembered that some of the most poetic and mystical writing in praise of the Mother of God has come from Western writers such as Bernard of Clairvaux, Pierre de Bérulle, and Louis Marie Grignion de Montfort, who flourished between the twelfth and seventeenth centuries, to name just a few.[8] As I

[8]M.-B. Saïd and G. Perigo, trans., *Bernard of Clairvaux, Magnificat: Homilies in Praise of the Blessed Virgin Mary*, Cistercian Fathers Series 18 (Kalamazoo, MI: Cistercian Publications, 1979); L.M. Glendon, trans., *Bérulle and the French School: Selected Writings* (New York and Mahwah: Paulist Press, 1989).

suggested in Chapter Eight, we must hope that ecumenical discussions exploring the similarities and differences between traditions will continue to take place.

In the course of this book, I have introduced a variety of themes connected with Marian doctrine and devotion in Orthodox Christianity. The approach that I have adopted has been largely historical, with perhaps greater emphasis on the early Christian and medieval periods than on the present. Traditions surrounding the Mother of God developed slowly in the course of the first Christian millennium, apparently because Church leaders were reluctant to describe this holy figure, about whom Scripture is strangely reticent, in too much detail. As they meditated on the biblical basis for apocryphal narratives, types, and metaphorical images in relation to Mary, these were slowly adopted into the liturgical life of the Church. The rich collection of hymns, prayers, and narrative material that is read daily in the services thus has the authority that comes from centuries of assimilation. Orthodox Christian reflection on the Mother of God succeeds in balancing God's physical manifestation in creation with the mystery of his being. Mary thus points towards the ineffable joining of divinity and humanity in the person of Jesus Christ.